Creative Sciencing

Experiments for Hands-on Learning

Alfred DeVito

Professor Emeritus of Science Education

and

Gerald H. Krockover

Professor of Science Education

School Mathematics and Science Center
Purdue University
West Lafayette, Indiana

Good Year Books
Parsippany, New Jersey

DEDICATION

This book is dedicated to all 21st century learners, including our grandchildren. We would also like to express our appreciation to Dr. Mary Ann Grobbel and Judith Adams from Pearson Learning for their editing contributions and excellent advice in producing this book.

Good Year Books

are available for most basic curriculum subjects plus many enrichment areas. For more Good Year Books, contact your local bookseller or educational dealer. For a complete catalog with information about other Good Year Books, please write:

Good Year Books

An imprint of Pearson Learning
299 Jefferson Road, P.O. Box 480
Parsippany, NJ 07054-0480

www.pearsonlearning.com

1-800-321-3106

Cover Illustration: Alicia Buelow
Book Design: Robert Dobaczewski
Design Manager: M. Jane Heelan
Editor: Mary Ann Grobbel
Executive Editor: Judith Adams

Fourth edition.

ISBN 0-673-58900-5

1 2 3 4 5 6 7 8 9 - ML - 06 05 04 03 02 01 00

This Book Is Printed
on Recycled Paper

WHY?

Creative Sciencing: Experiments for Hands-On Learning is a resource book for both preservice and in-service teachers. It is a valuable learning tool for the elementary science methods course, and it is a comprehensive source of ideas and activities for use in the intermediate-level classroom.

The organization of this book is based on several premises. One is that teachers want and need new, exciting science activities for their science programs. A variety of fresh, field-tested science ideas has been furnished. In Appendix A, these activities are cross-referenced according to the processes of science and the content area covered. These areas are also referenced to the National Science Education Standards.

More importantly, each activity is written to evoke ideas from the student, thus enabling each activity to serve as a springboard for further activities. This is the creative sciencing process that is featured in the "Brainstorming in Science" section.

Another premise is that teachers often have difficulty acquiring materials for successfully implementing science. The "Shoestring Sciencing" section of this book deals with doing more science for less money. "Creative Sciencing Recipes" includes useful recipes and projects that you can make with children. Appendices that provide metric conversions and sources for more ideas and activities with websites are also provided.

Numerous studies call for quality, hands-on science education experiences for children. Creative Sciencing will assist you in meeting this need. And, coupled with our companion textbook, *Activities Handbook for Energy Education,* a wealth of resources are at your fingertips.

We would like to thank the previous users of our books who for the past 24 years have supported and endorsed our creative sciencing approach to learning.

Alfred DeVito

Gerald H. Krockover

TABLE OF CONTENTS

Brainstorming in Science • BIS

Shoestring Sciencing • SS

Creative Sciencing Recipes • CSR

APPENDIX A

APPENDIX B

APPENDIX C

Brainstorming in Science

A Sneak Preview

Some of the nearly 100 sciencing activities in this section are confined to science. Many go beyond into other areas—social studies, mathematics, language arts, art, and music—that can encourage students to utilize science as a part of life as a whole, not as a separate entity.

Each investigation is introduced as a unit independent of the others. When the material warrants precautions for safety reasons, a **WARNING** is included.

The materials listed are per student or group of students. Although written for the students to do themselves, the activities can be done with the teacher, at your discretion. Some of the activities are written to give students experience with the process; others allow the students to draw conclusions.

Very few activities in science apply specifically to only one grade level. You must tailor the science investigation to your needs and the children's needs. A good example is the time-honored activity called "Why Does a Burning Candle Go Out?" BIS 1.

This could be used as a fourth-grade problem or it could be restructured into a suitable fifth, eighth, twelfth, or college-level investigation. What separates these instructional levels? In a fourth-grade class the teacher ignites the candle, places a jar over it, and waits. The students describe their observations. They may make several inferences. They may even propose tentative explanations. If you were teaching this activity at a higher level, you would probably need to extend it.

How does one extend an activity? That is what brainstorming is all about. BIS 1 addresses this problem by suggesting a basic introductory activity and extending this into MORE creative involvement at higher levels of problem-solving skills.

Think of as many ways of helping students to manipulate the material as you can. You have a candle, a match, a glass jar, some available air, and a surface on which the glass jar rests. Which variable could be changed? When brainstorming, don't cast out any idea as foolish until you have had a chance to examine it.

Brainstorming can produce a gentle trickle of ideas or an avalanche. Accept it either way; an idea is an idea. If you don't like it, you can always discard it later, but for the moment keep it. Who knows, it may germinate and flower into a useful idea.

When you are brainstorming, what could you do to extend the lesson even further? Brainstorming is a self-quizzing procedure, which invites you to ask many questions.

Most science activities can be quickly tailored for greater challenge by insisting on more rigor in the observing and quantifying that evolve from the activities. The amount of difficulty in the questions you ask is also important.

Specific pieces of equipment and the mathematical and language requirements that you impose on a learning situation can move a lesson from simplicity into sophistication. A ball rolling down an inclined plane may be a good observation activity. But introducing thermometers, timers, balances, protractors, and metric rulers where appropriate; requiring different degrees of accuracy; and using appropriate language arts activities can make this activity into one you can use to challenge older students.

There really is no end to the scope and directions in which creative sciencing can lead you if you are curious and willing to engage yourself and your students in this kind of thinking. The great range of applications makes it unnecessary to provide performance objectives and stated grade levels for individual activities in this book. You make the decisions; you alone put together the why.

Motivated teachers are always concerned that they teach well, that they are current with what is new and appropriate to their teaching, and that children enjoy, learn, and profit from the entire school experience. Hands-on science activities have been perceived as exciting, worthwhile science involvement for children—and they are—though they are only one facet of science education.

Questions to Ask When Engaged in Hands-On Science Activities

What are the objectives of the activity? Where does involvement with this activity lead? Is the end purpose of this activity content acquisition, concept development, or something else?

What skills, equipment, or materials are necessary to make this activity succeed?

Does this activity build on anything? Where have you been in science? Where are you now? Where are you going?

How does this activity fit into the mosaic structure of science? What is its place within your instructional program?

Did this activity evoke questions from children that warrant further investigations?

What opportunities exist for experimentation within the activity or as an outcome of this activity?

These questions need not be a checklist that precedes each hands-on science activity. Rather, they should serve as a periodic review to keep focused on the purpose of the activity and its relevance to the structure of science.

Acquiring Skills for Teaching Science

A teacher should acquire all the science content background possible. Because there is no substitute for knowing the content of science, content acquisition should be sustained throughout a teaching career. Content acquisition alone, however, will not fulfill the requirements necessary to qualify as a teacher of science.

Concomitant with the knowledge of content, a teacher should master the process skills of science. The processes of science provide the skills necessary for the orchestration of experimentation, which is a process unique to science.

A teacher should also become knowledgeable about the structural themes of science—such as the patterns of change and systems and their interactions. In day-to-day science instruction, the teacher should constantly search out relationships between the structural themes of science, as they are observed when instruction is provided in discrete science disciplines. This tie-in adds mortar to the bricks of content, concepts, generalizations, laws, and models.

A recommended method of science instruction should incorporate these and other facets or processes directed toward experimentation. Experimentation necessitates content knowledge, knowledge of the structure of science, experiences in hands-on science activities, and the creative search for solutions to questions that arise.

Excellent books are available that elaborate on one or more of the facets of science instruction.

A minimum of these three extremely useful publications are recommended for your library:

1. *Resources for Teaching Middle School Science*. National Science Resources Center, National Academy Press, 2101 Constitution Ave., NW, Washington, DC 20418 (Web address: http://www.si.edu/nsrc) This is an excellent comprehensive source book for teachers.

2. *Resources for Teaching Elementary School Science*. Available from the same source as *Resources for Teaching Middle School Science*. This is also a comprehensive source book.

3. *National Science Education Standards*. Also available from National Academy Press. (Web address http://www.nap.edu) This is an outstanding publication delineating science education standards.

Start small. Grow pursuing excellence. You and your students should experience and enjoy challenges and successes.

Continue to ask questions about science and science instruction. Challenge pedagogical dictates and resolve events enabling you to successfully teach science.

Teach the process skills. Mastery of the process skills is tantamount to successful participation in the skill of experimentation.

Search for connections relating what you are teaching to the structure of science.

ON TEACHING

Pour in equal parts of anticipation and preparation;

Add eight hours sleep for the teacher, before teaching;

Season with a sense of humor;

And use sufficient resourcefulness to keep the mixture from becoming lumpy!

Why Does a Burning Candle Go Out?

Materials: candle; aluminum pie plate; modeling clay; clear glass jar; matches; 2 wood blocks **More:** candles of various diameters; food-warmer candle; 3 birthday candles; matches; 3 soda straws; aluminum pie pan; modeling clay; glass jars of various heights and volumes; 1-gallon glass jar; thumbtacks; metal coffee can

Facts to know:

◇ Oxygen gas exists in air. A flame needs oxygen to burn.

◇ A burning candle gives off a gas called carbon dioxide. This gas does not keep a flame burning.

◇ Carbon dioxide is heavier than oxygen.

WARNING: A burning candle is dangerous. Have a fire extinguisher or a bucket of water handy in case a problem occurs. Do this activity only when an adult is present. With younger students, the teacher should light the candle for all activities.

Procedure:

❧ Use modeling clay to anchor a candle to the pie pan. Light the candle.

❧ Place the jar over the candle. Record the time it takes the flame to go out.

What did you observe?

Did the burning candle use all the oxygen in the jar?

Did you see or hear anything as the candle burned and then went out?

❧ Repeat the activity using modeling clay to seal the bottom of the jar so that nothing can come in or go out. Record the time it takes for the flame to go out.

What can you conclude about sealed versus unsealed jars and the length of burning time?

❧ Remove the clay seal. Use wood blocks to raise the jar off the bottom of the pie pan. Then pour water into the pie pan to seal the jar. Record the time it takes for the flame to go out.

What did you observe?

What happened to the water level?

Did the burning candle use all the oxygen in the jar? Devise a way to support your answer.

Is it possible that the candle drowned in its own carbon dioxide? How might you test this idea?

More:

- Use jars of different heights, volumes, and shapes to cover the burning candle. Vary the number and size of the candles. Float the food-warmer candle on water. (Place thumbtacks in the base of the candle to keep it floating upright.)

- Record the time it takes for the flame to go out in each case.

    Which variations affected the burning time of the candle—height, volume, or shape of container; size of candle, or number of candles?

    What happened to the burning candle floating in water? Did the flame go out immediately? Did the candle continue to burn? What happened to the candle as it continued to burn? Is carbon dioxide gas soluble in water? Design some action to support your statement. Remember that carbonated drinks contain carbon dioxide.

- Cut the soda straws into three different lengths. Place the base of 1 birthday candle inside each straw. Then anchor the straws in a straight line in modeling clay to keep them upright. Light the candles.

- Cover the lit candles with the 1-gallon glass jar. Predict which candle will go out first. Record the time it takes for each of the flames to go out.

- Repeat the activity with the straws arranged in a triangular pattern in the modeling clay. Record the time it takes for each of the flames to go out.

    In what order did the burning candles go out in each pattern?

    Can you explain your observations?

- Cover a burning candle with the coffee can.

    How can you determine when the burning candle goes out without using direct observation?

Related activities: BIS 21, BIS 30

BIS **2**

Garden in a Jar—Studying Seeds and Plants

Materials: vegetable seeds such as lima bean, mung bean, or corn (for quick growth choose mung beans; for easy handling of seed and plants choose lima beans); household bleach; paper towel; glass jar; vermiculite or other absorbent material; graph paper **More:** bean seed; mimosa plant

Procedure:

* Soak seeds in water overnight to speed up germination.

* Then soak the seeds in diluted household bleach for 10 to 15 minutes.

* Fold a paper towel into a cylinder. (The cylinder should be shorter than the height of the jar.)

* Place the cylinder in the jar. (Be sure the cylinder hugs the sides of the jar.)

* Pour vermiculite into the cylinder until it is half full.

* Pry the cylinder away from the sides of the jar and slip the seeds between the cylinder and the jar, arranging them as you like.

* Water the seeds by wetting the cylinder and vermiculite. Drain off any excess water.

* Place the jar in sunlight. Observe the jar daily and record your observations. Keep the cylinder and vermiculite moist.

    How long did it take your seeds to germinate? Compare your germination time with your classmates. What can you conclude?

    What happened to plants that dried out? Plants that were watered too much?

    What happened to a plant when portions were snipped off?

* Graph the growth of the plant over time. Graph the growth of various parts of the plant over time.

The mimosa plant is often called the sensitive plant. When you touch its leaves, they fold gently under your fingers. Mimosa leaves also fold at night and open again in daylight.

More:

* Soak a bean seed in water for 6 to 8 hours. Separate the two halves of the seed and look inside.

    Can you identify the parts of a plant—leaves, stem, and root system?

* Use the plant grown in the jar to examine plant reactions to one of these factors: geotropism, sound, electrical stimulation, magnetism, pressure, various soil types, varying degrees of salinity, and various amounts of fertilization.

    What materials do you need to test the plant's reactions?

    Plan an experiment using these materials.

* Touch a leaf on a mimosa plant.

    What do you observe?

* Place the mimosa plant in the dark for several hours. Look at the leaves. Then put the plant in sunlight and observe the leaves again.

    What did you notice about the leaves?

Related activities: BIS 24, BIS 43, BIS 58, BIS 78, SS 18.

A Milky Change or Surface Tension Swirls

BIS **3**

Materials: milk; aluminum pie pan; red, yellow, green, and blue food coloring; clear or white liquid dishwashing soap; metric ruler

Procedure:

* Pour milk into the pie pan to a depth of 2 to 2.5 cm.

* Carefully place drops of red, yellow, green, and blue food coloring spaced evenly on the milk.

* Squeeze the soap around the rim of the pie pan.

    What did you observe?

    Why do you think it happened?

Related activity: BIS 4

Measuring Surface Tension of Liquids

Materials: two 6-inch lengths and one 12-inch length of 1 x 2-inch wood; 4 x 4-inch wood block about 1-inch thick; nails; hammer; plastic container; plastic lid; 6-oz paper cup; paper clips; metal washers for weights; string; scissors; ruler; water (rainwater, tap water); vinegar; apple juice; cooking oil; metric balance **More:** several brands of liquid dishwashing soap; 3 plastic lids

Facts to know:

◇ When water molecules contact air or other matter, they squeeze together, forming a dense layer called <u>surface tension.</u>

Procedure:

❧ Construct an instrument to measure surface tension—a tensiometer—by nailing the 6-inch lengths of wood about 4 inches from one end of the 12-inch piece (see illustration). The 12-inch length should be between the two 6-inch pieces. (The tensiometer will have a long arm and a short arm.)

❧ Then nail the other end of the 6-inch pieces to the wood block so that the balance stands upright.

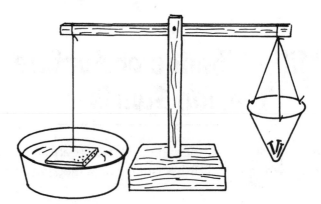

❧ Cut a 1-inch square from the plastic lid. Make a small hole in the center of the square.

❧ Suspend the square from the long arm of the tensiometer.

❧ Suspend a paper cup from the short arm of the tensiometer.

❧ The paper cup will outweigh the plastic square; use paper clips on the lighter side to make both arms equal in weight.

❧ Fill the plastic container with water and place it beneath the square on the long arm.

❧ Carefully push down on the arm until the square touches the water. Your tensiometer will now be out of balance. If you gently tap the opposing balance arm, you will feel a grabbing attraction between the square and the water. (This attraction is called *surface tension* and can be measured.)

- With the square in contact with the water, carefully add the metal washers to the paper cup. Record the number of washers needed to break the surface tension.

- Express surface tension in washers used per square inch, or weigh the washers on a metric scale to express the surface tension in grams per square inch.

- Repeat the activity with hot, lukewarm, and cold water in the container. Measure the surface tension with each.

- Replace the water in the container with other liquids, such as rainwater, vinegar, apple juice, and cooking oil. Measure the surface tension with each.

    Does the temperature of the water affect its surface tension?

    Do all liquids exhibit the same surface tension?

    How do they compare to one another?

More:

- Vary the geometric shape of the piece of the plastic, but keep the same surface area as the 1-inch square. Try measuring the surface tension with a 1 x 2-inch triangle, a $\frac{1}{2}$ x 2-inch rectangle, or a 1-inch-diameter circle.

    Does the geometric shape affect surface tension? Does it increase, decrease, or remain the same?

    Would a 2-inch plastic square require twice the measure of weights to break the surface tension? What about a 3-inch square?

- Add a few drops of liquid soap to the water in the container and measure the surface tension. Repeat with different brands of detergent. Again measure the surface tension.

    How does the soap affect surface tension?

    Which soap reduces surface tension the most?

Related activity: BIS 47

Let There Be Light and Color Too— Lenses, Reflection, Refraction

Facts to know:

◊ Lenses are transparent materials, such as glass, whose surfaces are not flat. Two major types are convex and concave lenses.

◊ Viewed in cross section, a convex lens is thicker in the middle than at its ends. A concave lens is thinner in the middle and thicker at its ends.

◊ A convex lens converges light that strikes its surface and passes through it. The light rays merge together at a point called the <u>focal point.</u> These same rays exit the focal point in a pattern similar to their original order, but inverted. So, images seen through a convex lens are upside down.

◊◊◊

As you move the lens from close to your eyes to farther away, you should see the tree magnified, then blurred in the focal zone, and, finally, inverted.

Materials: *Part One:* magnifying glass; clear cylindrical container; drawing of a tree; piece of wax paper; piece of newspaper; cooking oil; rubbing alcohol; glycerin; thick-bottomed drinking glass

Part Two: 5 x 8-inch index card; paper punch; flashlight; mirror

Part Three: 5 or 10-gallon aquarium; Styrofoam cup; flashlight; coin; clear plastic container **More:** comb; 5 x 8-inch index card; convex lens; concave lens; flashlight; 4-inch square of window glass with masking tape on all edges; white paper; black paper; 2 pocket mirrors; coin

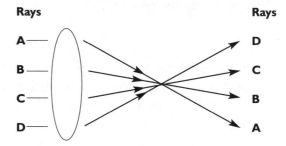

PART ONE: LENSES

Procedure:

• Look at the drawing of the tree through the magnifying glass and through the cylindrical container filled with water. (Both act as convex lenses.) While looking at the picture, move the lens closer to and farther from your eyes.

> *What do you observe happening?*

> *What happens when the lens is close to your eyes? When it is far away?*

• Place the newspaper on a flat surface and cover it with the wax paper. Then place a drop of water on the wax paper. Gently lift the wax paper. Observe the newsprint.

• Experiment with larger water droplets and different liquids— cooking oil, rubbing alcohol, and glycerin. Place a drop on the wax paper and then gently lift it. Observe the newsprint.

> *What happens to the letters in the newspaper as the wax paper is lifted?*

> *What happens with a larger drop of water?*

> *Will all liquid droplets provide the same level of magnification? Which provide the greatest magnification?*

- Place the drinking glass at eye level. Look through the bottom of the glass. (It acts like a concave lens.)

    What do you observe?

    Are objects magnified? Inverted?

PART TWO: REFLECTION _____

Procedure:

- Fold a 5 x 8-inch index card into 3 equal parts. In the center part, punch 4 holes about equal distance apart in a horizontal line.

- Darken the room. Place the index card in front of a flashlight so that the light beam can shine through all holes at the same time.

- Place a mirror in the path of the light at right angles to the light beams. Observe the reflected beams.

Light is reflected as it bounces off a polished surface such as glass. The angle of incoming light (<u>angle of incidence</u>) is always equal in degrees to the angle of outgoing light (<u>angle of reflection</u>).

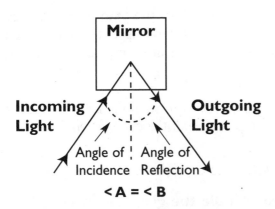

- Now turn the mirror at a different angle to the light beam. Observe the reflected beams.

    What do you observe about the individual beams coming from each hole?

    Do you observe that light beams are reflected off the mirror at the same angle that they strike the mirror?

PART THREE: REFRACTION _____

Procedure:

- Make a 2 x $\frac{1}{4}$-inch slot in the bottom of a Styrofoam cup. Place the cup over the head of a flashlight.

- Shine the flashlight straight down into an aquarium filled with water.

- Now shine the flashlight at an angle to the water surface.

    What do you observe about the light in each case?

When light passes obliquely from one material to another (such as air to water) it changes speed and direction. This change is known as <u>refraction,</u> or <u>bending.</u>

The white paper reflects the incoming light back through the glass. The light is diffused, however, making it difficult to see a clear reflection. Black paper absorbs the light passing through the glass. This allows you to see the light reflected from the glass.

* Place a coin on the bottom and near the edge of the plastic container. Look at the coin, then move to a new position where the coin disappears from your view. Remain there.

* Have someone slowly pour water into the container, leaving the coin in the same location. The coin should come into view.

    Why is the coin visible now? Has the coin really moved?

More:

* Cut a 1-inch diameter semicircular hole in the index card. Tape a comb across this opening.

* Stand the index card up on a table with the semicircular opening at the bottom.

* In a darkened room, shine a flashlight through the opening from the side opposite the comb. Observe the light-ray pattern as it passes through the comb.

* Now insert a convex lens into the path of the light as it exits from the comb. (For best results, raise up the index card so that the light rays go through the lens at its midpoint.)

* Repeat with a concave lens.

    What changes do you observe in the light-ray pattern with the convex lens in place? With the concave lens?

* Place the window glass on a sheet of white paper.

    WARNING: Handle the glass carefully.

* Observe your reflection in the glass.

* Now substitute black paper for the white paper.

    How do these two reflections compare?

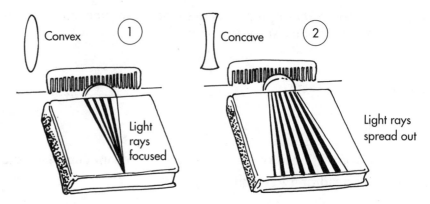

* Tape the pocket mirrors together, hinging them at right angles to each other.

* Stand the mirrors upright.

* Place the coin between the mirrors. Observe.

* Now change the angle between the mirrors.

    How many coins do you observe in each case?

    What happens when the angle between the mirrors increases? Decreases?

Related activity: BIS 54

The Dissolving Contest

Materials: hard candy such as Life Savers; stopwatch; clear cups
More: aspirin; soap powder; salt; penny; shoelace; leaves; clear cups

Procedure:

* Hold a whole-class dissolving contest. Pass out one candy to each student. On a signal from the leader, all students put the candy in their mouths. (Use only a whole candy; do not chew it.)

* Each student should signal, by raising a hand, when his or her candy is thoroughly dissolved.

* As the students raise their hands, record the elapsed time for each student. (Alternatively, call out the time every 15 seconds and have students individually record their dissolving time.) Compile the data on the chalkboard.

    Who won? Who placed second? Third? Who took longest?

    What was the average dissolving time? What was the range?

    Did girls dissolve the candy faster than did boys?

    What factors influenced the rate of dissolving?

* Drop a candy into a cup of water. Observe the candy and record the dissolving time.

    What affected the rate of dissolving?

    Can you relate the cup of water in this activity to your mouth in the dissolving contest?

    What part of the human body compares with the cup?

    What serves the same purpose as the water?

    Is temperature involved in both instances?

    Can motion affect the rate of dissolving?

    What human factors, which might speed up or slow down the rate of dissolving, would not be present in the cup of water?

Students will discover how dissolving is affected when exposed surface area is varied.

- Try using cold, warm, and hot water to dissolve the candy. Record the dissolving time for each.

- Drop a candy into a cup of water and stir the water until the candy dissolves. Record the dissolving time.

- Increase the surface area of the candy by crushing and cutting the candy into halves, fourths, and eighths. Record the dissolving time for each.

    In how many ways can you make a candy dissolve faster?

    Compare the rate of dissolving of a whole candy to the time it takes for two halves, four quarters, eight eighths, or a pulverized candy to dissolve.

    What do you observe? Record the data and graph your results.

    How would a different flavor of candy or one with another color affect your results?

More:

- In separate cups of water put an aspirin, a teaspoon of soap powder, and a tablespoon of salt.

    WARNING: NEVER put anything in your mouth that is being used in the science laboratory.

- Record the dissolving time for each.

- Try dissolving a penny, a shoelace, and leaves.

    How many household items can you name that will dissolve?

    What else will dissolve?

    Do a penny, a shoelace, or leaves dissolve?

    How long do you think it would take them to dissolve?

    Can you think how you might get them to dissolve faster?

    Why don't you dissolve when you take a bath?

    Does an ice cube dissolve or melt in a glass of water?

    Does an ice cube dissolve or melt in the air (on a plate, of course)?

    Is there a difference between melting and dissolving? Can things dissolve in air?

    Can you dissolve as much salt or sugar in a glass of water as you want to? What are the limits for each?

    Compare the formation of crystals with the process of dissolving.

Related activities: BIS 34, BIS 39, BIS 53

The Swinging Pendulum

Materials: string; weights such as metal washers of various sizes; masking tape

Procedure:

* Make a pendulum from a length of string and a weight. Tie the weight to one end of the string and suspend the pendulum by taping the free end of the string to a desktop. Swing the pendulum and observe its action.

* Replace the weight with weights of different mass. Swing the pendulum and observe.

* Try using shorter and longer pieces of string. Swing the pendulum and observe.

* Hold the pendulum at different angles. Then swing the pendulum and observe.

   What happens to the action of the pendulum in each case?

   Does the distance you pulled the weight out from the center influence your results?

Related activities: BIS 41, SS 2, SS 12

The length of string, the mass of the weight, and the angle of initial release affect the motion of a pendulum.

The Evaporative Cooler

Materials: 2 clay garden pots of equal size; 2 shallow bowls wide enough to hold clay pots upside down; thermometer, water; sponge

Procedure:

* Wet your finger and then blow on it. (It should feel cooler as the moisture evaporates.)

   Can you compare this to what happens when you step out of a swimming pool on a breezy day?

* Construct two coolers by turning each clay pot upside down and placing it in a bowl. Leave one cooler dry. Soak the other cooler in water and add water to the bowl.

* Place both coolers outdoors. Record the air temperature.

- After one hour, record and compare the temperatures under each clay pot.

    What can you conclude?

- On a low-humidity day, write your name on the blackboard using a wet sponge. Record the time it takes for your name to disappear.

- Repeat this action on a high-humidity day.

    How long did it take for your name to disappear?

    Compare the time it took on the low-humidity day versus the time it took on the high-humidity day.

Related activities: BIS 6, BIS 34, BIS 39, BIS 53

BIS 9

The Case of the Burning Cheese Puff—Investigating Calories

Materials: 3 cheese puffs; metric balance; metal juice can; measuring cup; thermometer; wire square; ring stand; paper clip; modeling clay; matches **More:** sugar cube; calorie chart

Students will determine the number of calories in a given substance.

Facts to know:

◇ Temperature is a measure of how hot or how cold an object is. Temperature is measured in degrees Fahrenheit or degrees Celsius.

◇ Heat is a measure of what makes objects get hot. Heat is measured in calories. These calories are similar to, but not exactly the same as, the calories you count when you're on a diet.

◇◇◇

Procedure:

- Pour 50 ml of water into the juice can.

- Place the wire square on the ring stand and the can on the wire square. Record the initial temperature of the water in degrees Celsius.

- Attach the cheese puffs to a bent paper clip and place the paper clip in a ball of clay for support. Place this under the juice can.

- Strike a kitchen match and light the cheese puffs.

    WARNING: Be careful not to burn yourself!

- After the cheese puffs have burned completely, record the final temperature of the heated water.

- Subtract the initial temperature from the final temperature; this is the temperature change. The volume of water (in milliliters) times the temperature change (in degrees Celsius) is the number of calories of heat provided by the cheese puffs to heat the water.

- Calculate the number of calories of heat given off by the cheese puffs to heat the water. (To manipulate the units for this problem, remember that the density of water is 1 gram per milliliter and the heat capacity of water is 1 calorie per gram degree.) Figure out how your units cancel so that you end up with an answer in calories.

- Check your final answer with a friend who has tried this investigation.

    Are your answers the same? Why or why not? What variables can you list that would account for any differences?

- Change your answer to kilocalories (diet calories). (It takes 1,000 calories to make 1 kilocalorie.)

    How many kilocalories of heat were given off by the burning cheese puffs?

More:

- Substitute a sugar cube (equivalent to one teaspoon of sugar) for the cheese puffs and repeat the activity.

    How many kilocalories of heat are given off?

    How does this compare to the kilocalories of 1 teaspoon of sugar on the calorie chart?

- Using the calorie chart, add up the number of kilocalories you consume in a day and in a week.

    How does your body use up the calories you swallow?

    Why do people who get plenty of exercise stay thin?

Related activity: BIS 39

Pill Bug Pedways or Isopod Ideas

BIS **10**

Materials: pill bugs (can be found under rocks or collected from the sidewalk at night; mealworms or earthworms work well too); box for pillbugs; ruler; thermometer; small plastic container

Procedure:

- Place pill bugs in the box. Observe and measure them.

    How large is the largest?

    How small is the smallest?

- Design experiments to answer the following questions. Assemble the necessary materials and conduct your investigations.

    Do pill bugs prefer high or low temperatures?

    Do pill bugs prefer light or dark areas?

    Can pill bugs see?

Pill bugs, called sow bugs or isopods, curl up into a little ball or "pill" when disturbed.

What do pill bugs like to eat?

Do pill bugs swim?

Can pill bugs differentiate between colors?

Will a pill bug move backward or sideways?

Can pill bugs hear?

Can pill bugs smell?

How do pill bugs communicate?

Compare your results with your classmates.

Are your results the same?

How do they differ?

Related activity: BIS 61

BIS 11

Examining Equilibrium

Materials: Pyrex test tube; 1-hole rubber stopper; 11-cm length of glass tubing; test tube clamp; heat source; glass container; food coloring; matches **More:** glass bottle; plastic soda straw; glass or metal bowl; food coloring; modeling clay; 2 identical drinking glasses; blotting paper; matches

WARNING: Protective eyeglasses should be worn to avoid any problems from accidental breakage of glass. Have a fire extinguisher or water handy. This activity should be done under adult supervision.

Facts to know:

⬦ Equilibrium is a state of balance between opposing forces in nature.

⬦⬦⬦

Procedure:

☞ Place a small amount of water in the test tube.

☞ Insert the glass tubing through the rubber stopper and cap the test tube tightly. (The glass tubing should extend 1 cm into the test tube and 10 cm outside the test tube.)

☞ Use the clamp to hold the test tube over a heat source. Bring the water inside the test tube to a rolling boil.

☞ Quickly and carefully invert the test tube.

☞ Carefully place the inverted test tube into the container with room temperature colored water.

What do you observe?

Why do you think this happens?

How does this relate to equilibrium?

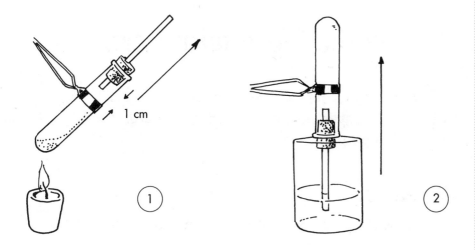

①   1 cm

②

More:

- Pour about a cupful of water into the glass bottle.

- Add a drop of food coloring to the water.

- Insert the straw into the water and let it extend above the top of the bottle.

- Seal the area around the straw from outside air with clay.

- Stand the bottle in the bowl. Observe the water level inside the straw.

- Pour warm (not boiling water) water over the bottle. Again, observe the water level inside the straw.

- Continue to observe the level of the water inside the straw as the system cools down.

    How is the water level in the straw affected as the water cools?

- Set the two glasses on a desktop. Wet a piece of blotting paper.

- Drop several lighted matches into one glass. Quickly place the wet blotting paper across this glass and invert the second glass directly over the first.

- With one hand positioned under the bottom of the first glass, to catch it if it is released, gently grasp the inverted glass and carefully lift the entire apparatus. (The two glasses should lift as one.)

    Why do the glasses stay together?

    Is the air pressure in the glasses the same as the air pressure outside the glasses?

Related activities: BIS 37, BIS 50, BIS 60, BIS 68, BIS 79

When the water in the test tube is heated, the expanding air drives some of the air out of the test tube. The air pressure in the test tube is reduced. The inverted, submerged test tube becomes a partial vacuum. Water shoots up into the test tube to restore equilibrium.

The burning matches reduce the air pressure in the glass. The wet blotting paper acts as a seal. This allows the partial vacuum caused by the cooling and contracting air inside the closed, two-glass apparatus to fill both glasses.

On the Move with Bernoulli

> **Materials:** plastic funnel; Ping-Pong ball **More:** quarter coin; $8\frac{1}{2}$ x 11-inch paper; pencil; 3 x 5-inch index card; candle with holder; round glass bottle; matches

Facts to know:

◇ The <u>Bernoulli principle</u>—
when the speed of air or a
liquid increases, there is a
decrease in pressure.

◇◇◇

Your breath creates
an area of low air
pressure on one side of
the ball and an area of
high pressure on the
other side of the ball.

Procedure:

⁕ Place the Ping-Pong ball inside the plastic funnel. Try to blow the ball out of the funnel.

> *How high can you blow the ball out of the funnel?*
>
> *Do huffs and puffs blow the ball out of the funnel?*
>
> *Do you find that the harder you blow, the more the ball stays in the funnel?*
>
> *When blowing into the funnel, where is the air speed the greatest? The least?*
>
> *Where is the pressure the least? The greatest?*
>
> *If you cannot blow the ball out of the funnel, in what area surrounding the ball is the pressure the greatest?*

⁕ Repeat the activity holding the funnel upside down with the ball nested inside the funnel. Blow into the inverted funnel. (Place the palm of your hand over the funnel until Bernoulli takes over.)

> *Why does the ball stay in the funnel? Can you blow it out of the funnel?*
>
> *Where is the pressure the least? The greatest?*

More:

⁕ Place the quarter about 1 inch from the edge of a flat desk.

⁕ Tip the bottle with its opening at a 45-degree angle to the desk, 1 inch above the desk, and about 1 inch behind the quarter.

⁕ Blow across the quarter parallel to the desk. (Keep trying. It takes a strong exhalation to move the quarter.)

> *Why does the quarter fly into the cup?*
>
> *Where is the pressure the least? The greatest?*

⁕ Fold an $8\frac{1}{2}$ x 11-inch paper in half horizontally and drape it over a pencil. Blow between the suspended paper halves.

> *What do you observe?*
>
> *How can Bernoulli's principle help explain your observations?*

- Make a bridge out of the index card by folding in $\frac{1}{4}$ inch on both of the 3-inch sides.

- Stand the bridge upright on a cleared desktop so that it is free standing and not touching another object. Try to flip the bridge over by blowing under the bridge.

  What happens when you blow harder?.

  How do your observations correlate with Bernoulli's principle?

  Explain why this simple task is difficult.

- Place the candle on a desk and light it.

  WARNING: A burning candle is dangerous. Have a fire extinguisher or a bucket of water handy in case a problem occurs. Do this activity only when an adult is present. With younger students, the teacher should light the candle for all activities.

- Place the bottle directly in front of the burning candle, close to the edge of the desk.

- Stand in front of the bottle and blow directly at it.

  What do you observe about the candle?

  Would this same effect occur if you used a square milk carton in place of the bottle?

Related activities: BIS 34, BIS 47, BIS 74

Sound Waves–Studying the Doppler Effect

BIS 13

Materials: alarm clock; 5-foot rope

Procedure:

- Tie the rope securely to the alarm clock.

- Set the alarm so that it rings constantly.

- Twirl the clock around you at eye level. (Make sure that everyone and everything is clear of your spin.)

- Listen to the pitch of the alarm.

  Do you notice that the pitch of the sound is higher as the clock swings toward you?

  What happens to the pitch as the clock moves away from you?

Sound waves from the alarm clock pile up as the clock moves toward you, resulting in a higher pitch sound. Once the twirling clock passes behind you, this piling up is reduced and the sound becomes lower. This is known as the <u>Doppler effect.</u>

Related activity: BIS 52

Action on the Rebound–Discovering Potential Energy

> **Materials:** old racquetball; sharp knife; meter stick; golf ball; Ping-Pong ball **More:** volleyball; Ping-Pong ball; golf ball

Procedure:

* Carefully remove about $\frac{1}{3}$ of the top portion of a racquetball using a sharp knife.

   > **WARNING: Cutting the racquetball is dangerous since it might roll as you try to cut it. Have an adult cut the ball.**

* Press in on the top of the $\frac{1}{3}$ portion to invert it so that the inside becomes the outside. (The piece now has a cuplike shape.)

* Hold this piece at shoulder height and let it fall to the ground.

* Observe the rebound.

   Where do you think the energy comes from to move this object up and through the air?

* Drop the Ping-Pong ball from a measured height. Measure and record the height of its rebound.

* Repeat with the golf ball, dropping it from the same height. Measure and record the height of the golf ball's rebound.

   Which object rebounds to the greatest height?

* Place the Ping-Pong ball vertically on top of the golf ball.

* Drop them simultaneously. (The two objects should drop as one in a vertical drop. This may take several tries to master the technique.)

   What actions do you observe?

   Do you observe that the Ping-Pong ball rebounded much higher than it previously did?

More:

* Make a stack of three spheres by placing the Ping-Pong ball on top of the golf ball which is on top of the volleyball.

* Drop them simultaneously. (The three spheres should drop as one in a vertical drop).

   What do you observe happening as these objects strike the floor?

Related activities: BIS 23, BIS 46, BIS 78

When the $\frac{1}{3}$ of the racquetball is inverted, it is placed under tension and has <u>potential energy</u>. When it is dropped and strikes the floor, the object goes back to its original shape, releasing the stored energy and rebounding vigorously.

The golf ball strikes the floor and reverses its velocity an instant before the Ping-Pong ball. The greater mass of the golf ball plus its upward movement are transferred to the Ping-Pong ball.

Stone Counts–Rock Samples from Glacial Till

BIS **15**

Materials: assorted gravel or sample of glacial till (if you live in a glaciated region contact the state geological survey or local conservation agent to find the nearest till); bedrock map of neighboring states (available from U.S. Geological Survey)

Procedure:

* Sift through the rock material, or glacial till, and try to identify the rock fragments. If you live in the Midwest, the seven most common rocks will probably be granite, sandstone, shale, limestone, basalt, chert, and coal. (In other parts of the country, check with the state geological survey or local conservation agent for information about the most common rocks.)

* From a sample of 100 rock fragments, determine the percentage that is granite.

* Try to find possible sources for the rock fragments you have identified by using a bedrock map of your neighboring states.

  How far away are these sources?

  How far might the glacier have traveled?

  Can you explain why the glacier would carry the rock fragments this far and then drop them?

Related activities: BIS 17, BIS 48

Facts to know:

◇ Glacial till is unsorted, unstratified drift laid down directly by melting glaciers. It is composed of rock fragments of all sizes, brought together randomly. The fragments range from tiny clay particles to boulders weighing several tons.

 ◇◇◇

Kindling Point or What's My Temperature?

BIS **16**

Materials: unwaxed paper cup; ring stand; wire screen; candle or burner; matches; water **More:** thermometer; paper cup

Procedure:

* Pour water into the paper cup until it is $\frac{1}{3}$ full.

* Place a wire screen on the ring stand. Set the cup on the wire screen.

* Heat the water with a candle or burner.

The paper cup will not burn as long as it contains water. The water absorbs the heat and does not allow the paper to reach its kindling point. Once the water has dissipated, the cup will burn.

WARNING: Wear safety goggles. A flame is dangerous. Have a fire extinguisher or a bucket of water handy. This investigation should be done when an adult is present.

What do you observe?

Why doesn't the cup burn?

More:

- Measure the temperature of the water and the outside of the paper cup. Record the temperatures.

  What do you think is the kindling point of paper?

  How could you find out?

Related activities: BIS 34, BIS 39, BIS 53

BIS **17**

Geologic Correlation by Insoluble Residues

Facts to know:

◇ Geologic correlation is an earth science term to explain how rock layers are related to each other.

◇◇◇

Materials: 2 samples of carbonate rock such as limestone from different locations (try to find samples within a 15-mile radius of your school); metric balance that weighs to the nearest 0.01 g; 1,000 ml beaker; 150 ml of 50% hydrochloric acid (prepare by adding 75 ml of concentrated acid to 75 ml of water—**Always add acid to water,** never the reverse); glass funnel; filter paper; glass flask; hand lens

WARNING: Wear safety goggles. This activity should be performed when an adult is present.

Procedure:

- Place about 25 g of rock in the 1000-ml beaker.

- Add the 50% hydrochloric acid in small amounts to digest the rock.

- Do not let the material foam over the top. (You may need to experiment with the quantity of rock and the amount of acid used to obtain maximum digestion.)

- Place a glass funnel in a glass flask. Place a piece of filter paper in the funnel.

- Once the rock has been digested, the insoluble residue will be deposited on the bottom of the beaker. Filter the residue by pouring the liquid that remains in the beaker into the filter-paper-lined glass funnel.

- Wash the residue with water several times to remove any remaining acid.

- Weigh the residue.

- Calculate the percentage of residue by dividing the mass of the sample by the mass of the residue and multiplying by 100.

- Repeat with the other samples of rock.

- Examine the residues with a hand lens and record your observations. (You may be able to identify siliceous material, pyrite, hematite, silicified bryozoans, gypsum, or clay.)

  Do the residues correlate with each other?

  Do residues from two nearby locations have similar results?

  What are the limitations of the data? What sources of error should be allowed?

  Is any additional information needed to obtain correlation, such as the color of the rocks collected, diagnostic fossils, or bedding characteristics?

Related activities: BIS 15, BIS 48

Adapted from Gerald H. Krockover, "Correlation by Use of Insoluble Residues." *Journal of Geoscience Education* (January 1971), pp. 29–30. By permission.

The Gravity of It All—Exploring Center of Gravity

BIS **18**

Materials: modeling clay, enough to make 2 racquetball-size spheres; 2 identical lead fishing weights; colored nail polish **More:** cardboard; string; 3 nails; 3 fishing weights; pencil; ruler; 2 identical forks; toothpick; potato

Procedure:

- Make 2 racquetball-size spheres out of clay.

- Cut each sphere in half. In one sphere, press a lead fishing weight in the exact center of the sphere. In the other sphere, insert the weight off-center near the outer edge of the sphere.

- Rejoin the 2 halves of each sphere, smoothing the clay back to a sphere.

- Place a drop of colored nail polish on the sphere with the off-center weight to distinguish it from the other sphere.

Facts to know:

- All objects have a point at which they are held in balance by the force of gravity. This point is referred to as its center of gravity.

◇◇◇

Each sphere rolls until its center of gravity is at its lowest point. If the center of gravity is at the center, everything is in balance as the sphere is rolled. The off-center sphere will roll until its center of gravity is at its lowest point and will then stop.

- Roll each sphere several times.

- Observe and describe how the rolling pattern of one sphere compares to that of the other.

    Do the spheres roll in a straight line or in an erratic manner?

    Which sphere does which?

    How does the location of the interior weights relate to their roll patterns?

More:

- Draw an irregular shape on the piece of cardboard.

- Cut out the shape and make three holes at random near the edge of the shape. Insert a nail in each hole.

- Tie a weight to a 12-inch piece of string.

- Hang the weighted line on the nail of one hole. (The suspended line acts as a plumb line.)

- Use a pencil and ruler to trace the line formed by the plumb line.

- Then hang the line from the next nail and trace that line.

- Finally, hang the line from the last nail and trace the line.

    What does the intersection of these three lines represent?

    Is this the center of gravity, or balancing point, of the shape?

    What is the center of gravity of a square? Of a circle?

- Pierce a small potato with the 2 forks, one on each side directly opposite each other.

- Notch one end of a toothpick and insert the other end into the bottom of the potato.

- Balance the apparatus on a string suspended between two chairs.

    Why doesn't the apparatus fall off the string?

    Where is the potato's center of gravity? Does this help the potato balance?

Related activities: BIS 14, BIS 23, BIS 46, BIS 79

Conserving Mass

 BIS **19**

> **Materials:** slice of bread; slice of apple; 4 raisins; glass jar with lid; metric balance

Procedure:

* Place the bread, apple, and raisins in the glass jar and seal.

* Weigh the jar.

* Place the jar aside for one month.

* Observe what happens to the materials in the jar during this time.

  What do you think happened to the total mass? Has it increased, decreased, or remained the same?

* Now weigh the jar and see how the actual weight compares to your prediction.

  Would the results be the same with different materials in the jar? Why or why not?

Related activities: BIS 23, BIS 33, BIS 71

Mass, Volume, and Displacement

 BIS **20**

> **Materials:** sand; 2 graduated cylinders; water **More:** ice cube; small plastic container and lid; metric balance; salt; small plastic bottle with cap; 35-mm film canister and cap; Alka Seltzer tablet divided into 16 equal pieces

Procedure:

* Pour some sand into one graduated cylinder until it is about $\frac{2}{3}$ full. Record the volume.

* Pour water into the other cylinder until it is about $\frac{1}{3}$ full. Record the volume.

* Slowly add the water to the sand, fully saturating the sand. If necessary, add more water to saturate. Record any additional water used. If you do not have to use all your initial amount of water, record what you have left over.

  What do you observe?

  What is the volume of the sand plus water? The volume of the air spaces in the sand?

Facts to know:

◇ <u>Volume</u> is a convenient measurement to use when comparing amounts of substances, particularly liquids, because liquids flow and take on the shape of their containers.

◇◇◇

More:

- Weigh the plastic container and its lid.

- Put an ice cube in the container and weigh it again. After the ice has melted, weigh the container once more.

  What can you conclude about the change in mass when ice melts?

- Now freeze the container and the water. Weigh the container and its contents after it is frozen.

  Has the mass changed? Has the volume changed?

- Pour salt into the cap of the plastic bottle until it is $\frac{1}{2}$ full. Weigh and record the mass.

- Pour water into the bottle until it is $\frac{2}{3}$ full. Weigh and record the mass.

- Determine the combined weight of the cap with the salt and the bottle with water.

- Now, pour the salt into the bottle and screw the cap on tightly. Weigh the bottle of salt and water.

- Shake the bottle.

- When the salt is completely dissolved, reweigh the container.

  Does the mass change because of the dissolving action?

  Does the volume change?

- Pour water into a 35-mm film canister until it is $\frac{1}{4}$ full.

- Weigh the canister, its cap, and a $\frac{1}{16}$ portion of the Alka Seltzer tablet. Record the mass of the total apparatus.

- Place the piece of Alka Seltzer into the canister, immediately cap it tightly, and place it back on the balance.

  WARNING: Do NOT use a larger piece of antacid. Do not point the canister containing the antacid at anyone. If too much antacid is used, there will be an excessive buildup of gas, and the cap will blow off the canister.

- Slowly loosen the cap. Record the weight of the cap, bottle, and its contents.

  How does this measure compare to the mass prior to the chemical reaction?

  What can you conclude?

Related activities: BIS 33, BIS 71, BIS 83

The water flows between the grains of sand and fills the empty spaces. The amount of water used is the sum of the air space between all the sand particles.

Putting Out the Flame—
Experimenting with Carbon Dioxide

Materials: 2-inch candle; 8- or 9-inch aluminum pan; carbonated beverage; matches; measuring spoons; glass jar; baking soda; vinegar

WARNING: A burning candle is dangerous. Have a fire extinguisher or a bucket of water handy in case a problem occurs. Do this activity only when an adult is present. With younger students, the teacher should light the candle for all activities.

Procedure:

- Place the candle in the middle of the pan. Light the candle.

- Slowly pour the carbonated beverage into the pan. (The more carbonated the drink, the better.)

    What happens to the flame? Why?

- Place 2 to 3 teaspoons of baking soda in the glass jar.

- Slowly add vinegar. (The baking soda and vinegar interact to form carbon dioxide.)

- When the reaction slows, add a bit more vinegar.

- Quickly place a lighted match close to the mouth of the jar.

    What do you observe happening to the flame? Why?

- Quickly place a burning candle in the pan.

- Slowly pour the gas out of the jar, directing it at the flame.

    What happens to the flame?

Related activities: BIS 1, CSR 13

Facts to know:

◇ Carbon dioxide is composed of one part carbon and two parts oxygen. The chemical formula is CO_2.

◇◇◇

Since carbon dioxide is heavier than oxygen, it will fall toward the flame and smother it.

Highways and Byways within Plants

Materials: celery stalk with leaves; knife; glass; water; food coloring; 4 plants grown under identical conditions (same type of soil, temperature, amount of sunlight, and amount of water); petroleum jelly

Procedure:

* Cut off 1 inch from the bottom of the celery stalk.

* Place the stalk into the glass with water. Add food coloring to the water.

* Set it aside for an hour.

* Remove the celery stalk and cut it crosswise into several pieces.

* Examine the cross sections of the stalk and the leaves.

    What do you observe in the stalk and leaves?

    Why does the food coloring travel through the stalk and leaves?

* Label the 4 plants 1 to 4.

* Apply petroleum jelly to the leaves in the following manner. Plant 1—Coat only the underside of all the leaves. Plant 2—Coat only the topside of all the leaves. Plant 3—Coat both the underside and topside of all leaves. Plant 4—Do not coat any part of the plant.

* Water all 4 plants with the same amount of water and follow the same watering schedule.

* Observe the plants each day.

    What happens to each plant? Explain your observations.

    Do you observe that plant 1 and plant 3 died?

    What can you conclude about the importance of the plant openings?

Related activities: BIS 2, BIS 21, BIS 24, BIS 43, BIS 58, BIS 78, SS 7

Small openings in the underside of leaves allow water to exit after the plant has extracted the minerals necessary for growth. Leaf openings also allow carbon dioxide into the plant. Carbon dioxide is needed in the process of photosynthesis to produce the sugar necessary for the plant's life.

Pressure, Area, Mass, and Weight

Materials: graph paper with cm divisions; pencil; white-pine wood block (dimensions should be in cm and in whole numbers); metric ruler; spring scale; equal arm balance **More:** graph paper with cm divisions

Procedure:

* Trace the outline of your hand on graph paper.

* Imagine that you have just completed a one-hand handstand. (The area of your traced hand would have supported your entire weight.)

* Approximate the number of square centimeters enclosed within the traced-hand outline.

* Divide your weight by the number of square centimeters. (This gives you the pounds per square centimeter of pressure you would have exerted on a surface if you had done that one-hand handstand.)

    Would you, if placed on a spring scale, weigh more at the poles or at the equator?

    Would the quantity of matter of which you are composed change? Would there be the same amount of you?

* Measure the length, width, and height of the wood block (in cm).

* Determine the mass of the block (in g).

* Determine the weight of the block (in newtons). A newton is equivalent to 0.224 lb.

    What is the volume (in cm³) of the block?

    What is the surface area (in cm²) of each face?

    What is the total surface area (in cm²) of the block?

    What is the density of the block? (The density of white pine is about 0.6 g/cm³.)

    If you cut the block in half, would the mass change?

    Would the density change?

    Weigh the block in three different positions. Does the weight of the block change?

* Trace the outline of the block in the three positions on graph paper. (In each, the same weight is distributed over a different area.

Facts to know:

◇ <u>Weight</u> is the common name for the measurement of the force of gravity on a specific mass. A spring balance is used to measure this gravitational attraction in newtons, or ounces. The same object measured on a spring scale at two different locations may have different weights.

◇ <u>Mass</u> is the measure of the quantity of matter in an object. The mass does not change or vary with location. Mass is usually determined by comparing the mass of an object with the mass of a known object using an equal-arm balance.

◇ <u>Density</u> is a measure of the amount of matter in a specific volume of space. Density is independent of size.

If an astronaut weighed 180 newtons on a spring balance on earth, his or her weight on the moon would be 30 newtons (approximately $\frac{1}{6}$ of that recorded on earth). This is because of the difference between the moon's and the earth's gravitational attraction.

BIS 24

The pressure that an object exerts depends on the area on which the weight of the object rests.)

What is the pressure per square centimeter for the block in each orientation?

In which case is the pressure per square centimeter the greatest? The least?

More:

* Trace the outline of one heel of your shoe on graph paper.

    If you balance your weight on one heel, what will the pressure be as distributed over this area?

    If you traced a spike heel of the shoe of a woman (again, balanced on one heel) who weighed 120 pounds, how might this explain why women's shoes occasionally leave heel marks in linoleum floors?

Related activities: BIS 33, BIS 71

Adapted from Alfred De Vito. "Understanding Pressure and Area," *Science Activities,* 6(4), December 1971, pp. 28–30. By permission.

Behold the Mold–Investigating Mold Growth

Materials: fresh and stale slices of bread (rye, whole wheat, white); slices of fruit (banana, peach, apple); 4 clean, empty baby-food jars of varying size with lids; paper plate; magnifying glass; water **More:** slice of bread

WARNING: Wash hands thoroughly after doing this activity and do not inhale the mold spores!

Procedure:

* Place a few drops of water into a baby-food jar and cap it. Add the same amount of water to a larger jar and cap it. Add more water to a third jar and cap it. Leave the fourth jar dry and cap it too.

* After several days, observe any mold that has grown. Compare your results with your classmates' results.

    What factors can you identify that contributed to the growth of this mold?

    Who grew the most mold? Which mold collection had the greatest variety of colors?

    Does mold grow in a dry baby food jar? Does mold grow in all moist jars?

Does the size of the jar make a difference?

How much water needs to be added? Will too much water slow down mold growth?

- Place slices of fresh bread and stale bread in several places in the classroom. After one week, examine the bread for mold growth. Compare your results with your classmates' results.

    Can you grow mold with any type of bread?

    Does rye bread grow better mold than wheat bread?

    Does fresh bread grow more mold than stale bread?

- Place slices of banana, peach, and apple on the paper plate. Observe the fruit daily and look for signs of mold. Record the time it takes for each fruit to grow mold.

    How long does it take fruit to get moldy?

    Does it take longer for peaches, apples, or bananas to mold?

    When does the mold begin to form? Before or after the fruit dried out?

- Examine the mold with a magnifying glass. Describe its growth pattern.

    Does mold grow taller? Does it spread over the object's surface? Is mold a plant?

    How do you think mold growth would be affected by light level and temperature?

More:

- Place a slice of bread in the dark. Observe it for mold growth. After two weeks, move the moldy bread to bright light.

    What observations can you make?

- Using what you have learned about mold, design an experiment to stop mold from growing.

Related activities: BIS 2, BIS 21, BIS 43, BIS 78

Heat Conduction

Aluminum conducts heat more quickly than iron. In general, metals that conduct heat best also conduct electricity best.

Materials: 3 aluminum nails; 3 iron nails; thin piece of Styrofoam (about 6-inch square); shallow aluminum tray; water

Procedure:

- Pour water into an aluminum tray and freeze.

- Press 3 aluminum nails and 3 iron nails through a piece of Styrofoam until the heads of the nails are against the Styrofoam.

- Place these nails in contact with the slab of ice in the tray. Predict the reactions that will take place between the nails and the ice.

  What do you observe happening? Was your prediction correct?

  Can you explain why water in a lake freezes first around the lake's edge?

  Why does ice melt first along the lake's edge in spring?

  Which loses heat faster in fall, land or water?

  Which gains heat faster in spring, land or water?

Related activities: BIS 34, BIS 62

Carbon Dioxide from Plants

Materials: 4 test tubes and stoppers; test-tube rack; water (from pond or aquarium); bromthymol blue; elodea (water plant available at pet stores); 2 small water snails **More:** goldfish; small fishbowl

Procedure:

- Fill the 4 test tubes with the pond or aquarium water to within 1 or 2 inches of the top. Label the test tubes from 1 to 4.

- Add 3 drops of bromthymol blue indicator solution to each test tube. (Bromthymol blue solution turns green if the water becomes acidic because of the presence of carbon dioxide.)

- In test tube 1 place a leafy portion of elodea; test tube 2— a small snail; test tube 3—a leafy portion of elodea and a small snail; test tube 4—leave empty.

- Tightly seal all 4 test tubes with stoppers and set them in strong light but not direct sunlight.

- Observe any changes.

   Do you think there are any changes in the presence or absence of dissolved carbon dioxide?

   How can you explain your observations?

More:

- Place a goldfish in a fishbowl. Observe the fish every day for 3 days.

   Does the goldfish act differently on day 3? Does it come to the surface to gulp air?

   Devise a method to give the goldfish more oxygen without changing the water.

Related activities: BIS 69, SS 11

Water plants added to a fishbowl will supply oxygen. In the process of photosynthesis, the plant manufactures its own food from carbon dioxide, water, and sunlight and creates oxygen.

Heat Energy, Temperature, and Calories or Check Your Pot

BIS **27**

Materials: 2-quart cooking pot; 2-gallon cooking pot; stove; thermometer; 2 small metal cans; ice cubes; clock or watch
More: graph paper

WARNING: Be careful around heat to prevent burns. Do this activity only when an adult is present.

Procedure:

- Pour 1 quart of water into the smaller pot, and 1 gallon of water into the larger pot.

- Place the 2 pans of water on stove burners.

- Bring the water in both pots to a boil. Measure the temperature of the water in each pot when it reaches the boiling point and record the temperature.

- When the water is boiling, add a metal can filled with ice cubes to each pot. Count how many ice cubes melt in each pot after 1 minute, 2 minutes, and 5 minutes.

   Were both pots of water at the same temperature when the water was boiling?

   How many ice cubes melted in the small pot? In the large pot?

   Can you explain the results?

Facts to know:

◇ Heat is measured in calories. A <u>calorie</u> is the amount of heat needed to raise one gram of water one degree Centigrade. These calories are called small calories to distinguish them from food Calories. One food Calorie is equal to 1,000 small calories.

◇◇◇

The larger pot of water needs more heat to bring it to a boil. It has more heat energy to give up to the ice cubes, so more ice cubes melt in the larger pot.

More:

* Make a graph of temperature change over time for the small pot and a similar graph for the large pot.

  What did you observe about the two graphs?

  What predictions can you make?

Related activities: BIS 1, BIS 11, BIS 12, BIS 13, BIS 14, BIS 25

BIS 28

Why Does a Burning Match Curl Up?

Materials: wood kitchen matches; paper matches

Students will be stimulated by astute observations and work through an explanation of an observed phenomenon.

WARNING: Have a fire extinguisher or bucket of water handy in case a problem develops. This activity should be done only when an adult is present.

Procedure:

* Light a kitchen match and hold it steady in a horizontal position.

* Observe it burning.

* When the flame is near the end you are holding, blow it out.

  How many of your senses did you involve in your observation?

  What did you notice?

  Did you notice that the wooden kitchen match burned under these conditions curled upward?

* Repeat the activity several times to check.

* Repeat the activity with a paper match.

* Compare your results with your classmates' results.

  How many matches curl upward?

  Do all matches, including paper matches, curl up? If not, then perhaps wooden kitchen matches have something unique that causes the observed result. Do you know anything about wood that might lead you to an explanation?

  What bearing does holding it horizontal and not rotating the match have on the result?

  Would the match curl sideways if it were held vertically? If it were rotated?

  When the match burns, where is the hottest portion of it? The lower or the top portion? Which portion do you think burns more completely?

What other objects bend or curl when light or heat is applied to them? Have you ever observed a plant bend toward the light? Have you ever observed a bimetallic strip react to heat?

Can you use this information to offer a possible explanation of why a burning match curls up?

Related activities: BIS 33, BIS 34, BIS 69, BIS 74

Temperature Changes and Air

Materials: balloon; measuring tape; thermometer **More:** thermometer; glass jar (large enough for thermometer to fit in side); can of frozen liquid, fruit juice, or water; piece of a balloon; rubber bands

Procedure:

- Inflate the balloon and seal it.

- Measure the diameter of the balloon. Record the temperature of the room.

- Place the balloon inside a refrigerator for about 1 hour.

- Remeasure the diameter of the balloon.

    How do the two measures compare? Why do you think it happens?

More:

- Place the thermometer in the jar. Seal the jar by stretching the piece of balloon across the top. Fasten the piece with rubber bands.

- Observe the action of the balloon piece as the jar is placed in direct sunlight, shade, and inside a refrigerator for 1 hour.

- Record the temperature under each condition.

    How do the temperatures you measure compare with your observations about the balloon?

- Place a can of frozen liquid on a countertop to thaw. Observe the can and liquid as it thaws.

    Do you observe that the liquid appears to thaw from the top down? Why?

Related activities: BIS 14, BIS 31, BIS 67, BIS 83, SS 14

The frozen liquid in the container chills the surrounding air. This air is more dense than room-temperature air and sinks. The warm air that replaces the sinking cooler air thaws the upper portion of the jar first.

Volume, Displacement, and Diffusion

> **Materials:** clear glass jar; colored marker; golf ball; metric ruler; water **More:** egg; white vinegar; clear container; distilled water

Facts to know:

◇ <u>Diffusion</u> is the movement of something from an area of greater concentration to an area of lower concentration until equilibrium is reached.

◇ ◇ ◇

A semipermeable membrane under the shell of an *egg* selectively controls what goes in and what goes out. The distilled water diffuses across the semipermeable membrane.

Procedure:

* Pour water into the jar until it is half full. Mark the water level on the jar with a colored marker.

* Place the golf ball in the water.

* Mark the new water level on the jar.

* Measure the difference in centimeters between the two water levels. The difference is the volume of the golf ball.

* Convert the volume into cubic centimeters (cc). (Remember, 1 ml of displaced water is equivalent to 1 cubic centimeter.)

    How can you check your answer? Devise an experiment to check it.

More:

* Use the displacement method to determine the volume of an egg. (The same technique you used with the golf ball.)

* Then, place the egg in a container and cover it with white vinegar. Observe the eggshell throughout the day. Record your observations.

* Leave the egg in the vinegar for 24 hours. The shell will be completely dissolved. The interior of the egg is now contained only by a membrane.

* Pour off the vinegar, rinse the egg, and determine the volume of the egg without the shell.

* Submerge the egg in a solution of distilled water. Over 7 days, remove the egg daily to determine its volume, using the displacement method. Each time, return the egg to a container of fresh, distilled water.

* Record your volume calculations on a graph plotting time versus volume.

    What do you observe happening on the seventh day? Can you explain why it happened?

Related activities: BIS 20, BIS 23, BIS 34, BIS 71

The Water Cycle, the Water Cycle, the Water Cycle

Materials: 2 identical beverage cans, 1 at room temperature, 1 refrigerated; equal-arm balance **More:** drinking glass; ice; water; teakettle; metal spoon; oven mitt; burner or stove

Procedure:

- Place the 2 beverage cans on an equal-arm balance, one on each arm. Balance the apparatus.

- Describe what you observe.

    Do you observe that the balance arm with the cold can sinks?

    How do your observations relate to the water cycle?

    How do your observations relate to warm- and cold-weather fronts?

More:

- Place the glass with water and ice in it on a desktop. Observe the outside of the glass.

    How do you explain your observation?

    WARNING: This activity involves steam and heat. It should only be done under adult supervision.

- Boil water in a teakettle so that you can produce steam.

- Wearing an oven mitt for protection, place the metal spoon over the steam that is escaping.

    Where does the water come from?

    Discuss your inferences.

Related activities: BIS 14, BIS 29, BIS 67, BIS 83, SS 14

Facts to know:

◇ Water evaporates. This evaporated water is in the air around us in the form of water vapor.

◇◇◇

Cool air cannot hold as much water as warm air. Some of the water vapor condenses on the can as water droplets. The cold can becomes heavier and the balance arm sinks.

Pinto Bean Radioactive Decay

Materials: bag of pinto beans; shoebox with cover; graph paper **More:** 100 pennies

Procedure:

- From a bag of pinto beans select 100 at random and put them in a shoebox.

- Mark one inside wall of the shoebox with a dot.

- Assume that each pinto bean represents 1 atom of the radioactive element called "bean."

- With the lid on, shake the box for 10 seconds, which could represent a span of time in years.

- After the first 10 seconds, remove all the beans that have their black spot pointing in the direction of the dot. These beans represent atoms of the element bean that have decayed.

- Record the number of active atoms that remain in the box.

- Shake the box again, removing the beans that have their black spot pointing toward the dot. Record the new number of active atoms.

- Continue this procedure until all the beans have been removed from the box.

- Construct a graph of your data showing the rates of radioactive decay for bean.

  What is the half-life (when 50 are left) of the element bean?

  Did you get the same results as your classmates? Why or why not?

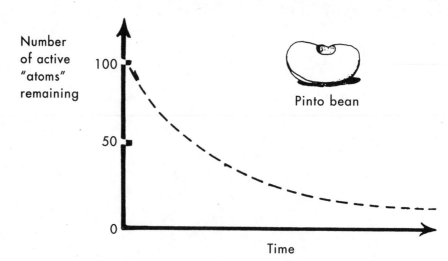

Pinto bean

More:

- Place 100 pennies in the shoebox, head side up.

- Shake the box as before, removing the pennies that are tail side up.

- Continue until all the pennies have been removed from the box.

  How does the half-life using pennies with a head or tail possibility differ from using pinto beans and their orientation toward the dot?

  What other objects could you use in this activity?

Related activities: BIS 35, BIS 61

The Cartesian Diver

Materials: clear bottle with cork; drinking glass; dropper; water
More: wood match; knife; metric ruler; clear bottle with cork; water

This activity reinforces the idea of cause and effect as air pressure is altered.

Procedure:

- Fill the drinking glass with water.

- Put the dropper in the water and see if it floats upright.

- Take up some water into the dropper. Add or remove water from the dropper until it barely floats. (Too much water will cause the dropper to sink to the bottom; too little water will make the dropper difficult to submerge.)

- Fill the clear bottle to the very top with water.

- Put the dropper containing water in the bottle. Place the cork on the bottle and press down slowly on the cork. (Stand back; excess water may squirt out.)

- Stop pressing on the cap.

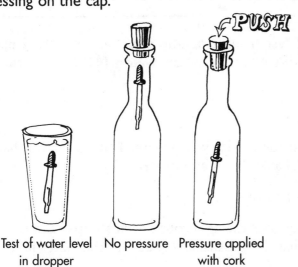

Test of water level   No pressure   Pressure applied
   in dropper   with cork

How can you explain this action and reaction? What happens to the water level inside the dropper as it changes position in the bottle?

Which is heavier, air or water?

When is the air inside the dropper compressed the most?

When the air is compressed, does the dropper contain more water, less water, or the same amount?

In which position do you think the dropper and its contents weigh the most?

Why does the dropper come back up when the pressure is released?

More:

- Cut off a 7 to 8-mm segment of the match, including the head and wood behind the head. (You may need to experiment with the length because matches vary from manufacturer to manufacturer.)

- Put this small portion of the match into the bottle filled with water.

- Cork the bottle and press firmly on the cork. (The match reacts to the pressure just like the dropper.)

  Is the explanation for this behavior and that of the dropper the same? Are the same components involved?

  When the match is at the bottom of the bottle, is it heavier than it was at the top of the bottle? How does it get heavier?

  How many variations of the Cartesian diver can you construct?

Related activities: BIS 23, BIS 40, BIS 69, BIS 74

BIS 34

Where Did the Water Go? Exploring Dissolving and Displacement

Materials: 2 test tubes; 2 one-hole rubber stoppers, 2 pieces of glass tubing 10-cm long; rock salt; water **More:** table salt; sugar

Procedure:

- Fill the 2 test tubes with warm water. Make sure they have identical water levels. Label one A and one B.

- Add rock salt to tube B.

- Put a piece of glass tubing through each stopper and cap each tube. Make sure that the glass tubing goes into the water in the test tube.

- Adjust the water levels so that both tubes are still identical by pushing the tubing in or out of the water.

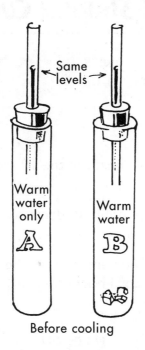

Before cooling

What do you predict will happen?

Will the water level rise because the rock salt melts? Will the water level fall?

Will the water level stay the same because the rock salt will not melt?

- After 1 hour observe the water level in the test tubes.

  What happened to the water level? Where did the water go?

- Make a hypothesis about what you observed.

  Did the water level go down because a gas was produced? Or did the water evaporate?

  Did the salt absorb the water? Did the water absorb the salt?

  Design an experiment to find out where the water went.

More:

- Repeat the activity with table salt or sugar instead of rock salt.

  Did you get the same results?

  Do you think you would get the same results if you used 2 liquids, such as rubbing alcohol and water, instead of water and salt? Why or why not?

Related activities: BIS 18, BIS 19, BIS 39, BIS 65, BIS 69, BIS 71

Adapted from Gerald H. Krockover, "Where Did the Water Go?" *Science Activities* (January 1973). pp. 38–39. By permission.

Normal Variation–The Bell-Shaped Curve

Materials: 10 lima beans; metric ruler; graph paper **More:** large plant; ruler; graph paper

The graph from data collected when one measures a characteristic in a population will be normally distributed, tracing a bell–shaped or normal curve.

Procedure:

* Measure and record the length of the 10 lima beans to the nearest millimeter.

* Exchange data with four other students so that you each have 50 measurements.

* Tally all the data. In millimeters, arrange the data from smallest to largest measure and record how often each measure occurs.

* Plot this information on a graph.

    How many beans that might be called extremely small did you have? How many extremely large ones? How did these two figures compare?

    How many so-called normal lima beans were counted?

    How did your curve from the lima-bean measurements differ from an ideal normal-shaped bell curve?

    If you measure another characteristic of the lima bean, do you think that your graph would have the same shape?

More:

* Measure the length or width of 10 leaves on a large plant.

* Plot this information on a graph.

    Was this graph the same shape as the graph of the lima beans? Can you explain why?

Related activities: BIS 32, BIS 61

Under Water and Under Tension— Surface Tension

Materials: clear drinking glass with wide mouth; aluminum tray; pennies; water **More:** pepper; toothpicks; soap bar; bowl; cooking oil; rubbing alcohol; dropper; 4-inch piece of thread; aluminum screening; clear drinking glass; BBs; water

Procedure:

- Fill the glass with water to the very top.

- Place the glass on the tray to catch any water overflow. (The glass should be thoroughly dried before and after filling it to the brim.)

- Predict how many pennies you can add to the glass before the water overflows.

- Observe and describe any changes in the water surface as more and more pennies are added to the glass.

    What did you observe about the surface water in the glass before it overflowed? Why did it happen?

    How many pennies were you able to get into the glass before the water overflowed?

More:

- Dip one end of the toothpick into the soap bar. Place the toothpick in the bowl half filled with water.

    What did you observe? What caused the toothpick to move?

    Do you think that the soap affected the toothpick?

- Sprinkle some pepper on water in the bowl.

- Dip one end of the toothpick into the soap bar.

- Touch the soapy end of the toothpick to the surface of the water in the middle of the bowl.

    Why do you think that the pepper particles moved? Did soap affect the surface tension?

- Pour water into the glass. Carefully add a drop of cooking oil.

- Slowly add rubbing alcohol to the glass with the dropper, allowing it to flow down the interior wall of the glass.

    What did you observe? Why did it happen?

    Do you think that the alcohol changed the surface tension?

Alcohol is less dense than water and oil. When alcohol is added, the oil is in contact with the surface tension of the alcohol. As the oil droplet tries to reach equilibrium, it gyrates.

- Make a loop with the 4-inch piece of thread.

- Place the loop in a bowl of water.

- Dip one end of the toothpick into a soap bar.

- Touch the toothpick to the surface of the water within the thread loop.

  What did you observe?

  Can you explain your observations?

  Where is surface tension greatest? Least?

- Construct a rectangular boat out of aluminum screening. Gently place this on the surface of water in the glass.

  Why didn't the boat sink? What did you notice about the area between the screen's wire strands?

  How much mass can your boat support before exceeding the ability of the surface-tension skin to support it?

- Carefully place BBs, one at a time, into your boat until the surface tension is broken and your boat sinks.

- Measure the bottom of your boat. Calculate the surface area of the bottom. Record the number of BBs it took to sink a boat of this measured surface area.

- Construct another screen boat with twice the bottom surface area of your first boat.

- Predict how many BBs are necessary to sink this second boat.

- Carefully place BBs in the boat until it sinks.

  How did this number of BBs compare to the number required to sink your first boat?

- Construct a third boat whose bottom surface area is three times that of your first boat.

- Again, predict how many BBs are necessary to sink this third boat.

- Carefully place BBs in the boat until it sinks.

- Compare the number of BBs necessary to sink each of the boats.

  What observations can you make about surface area and surface tension?

Related activities: BIS 3, BIS 4, BIS 20, BIS 23, BIS 30, BIS 40

Inclined-Ramp Rollers—Discoveries with an Inclined Plane

Materials: board (wood, Masonite, cardboard); steel ball bearing; Ping-Pong ball; marble; toy car; weights; metric ruler; timer; books
More: spherical objects of various weights; toy car; Ping-Pong ball; cooking oil; wax; fabric to cover board (corduroy, silk, or cotton); glue; sand; playground slide; metric ruler; timer

Procedure:

* Construct an inclined plane with the board. (Stack some books beneath one end of the board.)

* Mark off the board in centimeters so that distances can be measured. (Extend the measurements beyond the plane.)

* Roll the ball bearing down the plane. Record the time it takes to move through a specific distance.

* Calculate the speed (speed equals the distance divided by the time it takes to travel this distance).

* Roll the Ping-Pong ball and then the marble down the plane.

    What happens if you keep the size constant and vary the mass?
    What happens if you keep mass constant and vary the size?

* Roll the toy car down the plane. Add weights to the car and continue to roll it down the plane.

* Record and graph speed as the weight is increased.

* Place a loose object in the car and place several heavy books in the path of the car. Roll the car down the plane.

    What happens to the loose object?

More:

* Roll a spherical object down the inclined plane. Place a lighter, heavier, or same-size sphere in its path. Let them collide.

* After impact, record the distance and direction traveled by both objects.

    What happens when a heavier object hits a lighter object? When a lighter object hits a heavier object?

    How does this collision relate to a rushing fullback and a waiting stationary linebacker?

    What happens when you change the elevation of the plane?

Students will observe and record the effects of manipulating variables.

- Wax the surface of the inclined plane, or use different materials such as corduroy, silk, or cotton to cover it.

- Roll the Ping-Pong ball down the plane.

- Measure the time it takes the ball to go a specified distance.

  How does the texture of the plane affect the speed?

- Roll a sphere in oil. Roll it down the plane.

- Place glue on the wheels of the car, roll it in sand, let it dry, and then run it down the plane.

  How do these changes affect the speed?

- Repeat the above activities using a playground slide as an inclined plane.

  How do your results compare? Do you observe any difference in speed?

Related activities: BIS 41, BIS 60, BIS 77, BIS 79, SS 2

BIS 38

Rotational Inertia

Materials: 2 metal peanut or coffee cans with 4 plastic lids; 8 nails longer than the height of the containers; board; books; meter stick
More: protractor; same cans with lids; same nails

The <u>rotational inertia</u> of the can with the nails positioned near the rim is greater than that of the can with the nails grouped at the center. The can with the greater rotational inertia starts slowly but is more difficult to stop.

Procedure:

- Cut off both the tops and the bottoms of the cans. Place the lids on both ends of the cans.

- Push 4 nails through each lid. In one container, place the nails close to the center; in the second container, place the nails close to the rim.

- Make an inclined plane from a board and books. Place both cans at the top of the plane. Roll both cans down at the same time.

- Observe the cans as they roll down the plane. Measure and record the distance that each can traveled.

  Which can reached the bottom first?

  Which can, after leaving the incline, rolled the greatest distance?

  How can you explain these results?

More:

- Vary the angle of the inclined plane. Try 15 degrees elevation, 30 degrees elevation, and 45 degrees elevation.

- Roll the cans down the plane at each elevation. Record the distance the cans traveled.

    Did increasing the angle of the plane alter the results? Why or why not?

- Change the location of the nails on 1 can. Place 2 nails in the center of the lid and 2 nails close to the rim.

- Roll the can down the plane. Measure the distance the can traveled.

    Did moving the nails change the results?

Related activities: BIS 37, BIS 46, BIS 65

Which Antacid? Gas Generation from Antacid Tablets

BIS **39**

Materials: flask; 1-hole rubber stopper; aluminum pan; glass tubing; drinking glass; plastic tubing; 2 rubber erasers; masking tape; 3 x 5-inch index card; antacid tablet; water **More:** different brands of antacid tablets

Procedure:

- Construct a gas-collecting system as shown in the diagram.

- Insert a piece of glass tubing through the rubber stopper of the flask and seal the flask. Attach one end of the plastic tubing to the glass tubing and the other end of the tubing into the aluminum pan.

- Place the 2 erasers in the pan. Pour enough water into the pan to cover the erasers.

- Attach a piece of masking tape to the side of the drinking glass, running from the bottom to the top. Mark off the tape in centimeter and half-centimeter units for measuring the volume of the gas.

- Fill the glass to the brim with water. Place the index card over the mouth of the glass. Press firmly against the card and glass with one hand and invert the glass. (Do this over a sink—at least for practice runs.) You should feel the card adhering to the inverted glass of water.

* Move the inverted glass over to the pan. Remove your hand and lower the glass into place. When the glass is under the water and over the erasers, slip out the card and lower the glass.

* Position the hose under the inverted glass.

* Put a little water in the flask. Drop in $\frac{1}{4}$ tablet of antacid.

> **WARNING: Be careful! Remember any gas built up in a closed system may be dangerous. Keep the hose clear!**

* Observe the reaction in the flask, the gas bubbles within the inverted glass, and the water displaced by the gas.

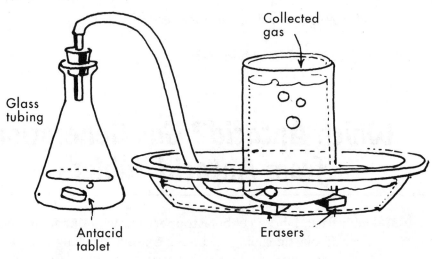

Rubber stopper (one hole)

Collected gas

Glass tubing

Antacid tablet

Erasers

Can you measure the amount of gas collected?

How did the amount of gas collected vary with different amounts of antacid?

Graph the results using $\frac{1}{8}, \frac{1}{4}, \frac{3}{8},$ and $\frac{1}{2}$ of the tablet.

Was any gas lost? Did the gas combine with the water? How would you find out?

More:

* Try hot, cold, or lukewarm water in the flask. Repeat the activity. This time record the amount of time it takes to dissolve the antacid and the amount of gas collected.

  Does changing the temperature affect the results?

* Compare equal amounts of different antacids. Repeat the activity with each.

  Which appeared to be the best generator of gas? Which was the best antacid?

Related activities: BIS 45, BIS 53

Comparing Densities with a Straw Hydrometer

Materials: clear plastic soda straw; melted sealing wax; metric ruler; waterproof marker; BBs; sand; 4 drinking glasses; olive oil; syrup; rubbing alcohol; water **More:** salt water; distilled water; glass jar with lid; motor oil; popcorn oil; cardboard; candle; small rock; ice cube

Procedure:

* Use the metric ruler and a waterproof marker to mark the straw in centimeter and half-centimeter units. (The straw is your hydrometer.) Seal the bottom of the straw with sealing wax.

* Place some BBs, plus sand if necessary, in the bottom of the straw.

* Put the weighted straw in a glass $\frac{3}{4}$ full of water.

* Adjust the BBs and sand so that the straw floats upright in the liquid. Mark the level of the water on the straw, labeling it 1. This is the density reference point for water.

    What does it mean if "1" is clearly visible above the liquid level when the straw is floating in a liquid other than water? When the number "1" is below the surface of another liquid?

* Fill the other glasses with syrup, alcohol, and olive oil. Place the hydrometer in each liquid. Observe the level of the liquid on the straw hydrometer.

    Is the level of the liquid the same as when the hydrometer was floating in water?

    Can you infer which liquid would float on water? Sink below water?

    Prove your inferences.

More:

* Check the level of the hydrometer in salt water, distilled water, warm water, and ice-cold water.

    Do they all have the same densities?

* Leave the hydrometer in salt water for a day or two.

    Does the density change?

* Try a density cocktail. Put some motor oil, popcorn oil, and water into a jar, almost any amount of each will do. Add one piece of cardboard, two pieces of paraffin from a candle, and a small rock. Shake this mixture and let it stand.

    Can you predict the sequence of liquids as they settle out? Which will be on top? On the bottom?

Facts to know:

◇ Water has a density of 1.0 g/cm^3, or 1. Things less dense than water float; things more dense than water sink; things equal in density to water barely submerge and do not sink.

* Place an ice cube in a glass containing cooking oil.

    Can you infer what will happen? Describe your observations.

    How can this be related to the movement of ocean currents?

Related activity: BIS 83

The Pendulum, or the Person on the Flying Trapeze

BIS 41

Materials: meter stick; two chairs; string; lead fishing weights; 3 cup hooks; 2 identical small bottles; sand; wood dowel; clock or watch with a second hand **More:** coil springs of different sizes; plastic birds of various sizes

Procedure:

* Place a meter stick across the two chair backs. Screw 3 cup hooks into the meter stick. (The hooks should be near the middle of the stick, about 2 or 3 inches apart.)

* Attach a weight to a string and hang it from 1 cup hook.

* Set the weighted string, or pendulum, in motion. (Swing the weight into an arc of approximately 30 degrees toward you and let go.) Record the time it takes for the pendulum to stop swinging.

    How long did it continue to swing?

* Hang two similar pendulums (on equal lengths of string) from 2 cup hooks on the meter stick.

* Let one remain at rest and swing the other into an arc of approximately 30 degrees.

    What happens to the stationary weight when the moving weight collides with it?

    What happens when you raise both weights and release them simultaneously? (Swing both weights into an arc of about 30 degrees so that the weights hit each other head-on.)

    What do you think will happen if one weight is greater than the other?

* Suspend two bottles filled with sand from 2 cup hooks on the meter stick. Cut a notch in each end of the wood dowel and attach the dowel to the strings of both bottles so that the dowel is between them. (The dowel should be placed close to where the strings attach to the meter stick.)

- Start one bottle swinging. Watch what happens to both bottles.

    What did you observe? How can you explain it?

More:

> **WARNING: Coiled springs can be dangerous if stretched too far.**

- Attach the plastic bird to one end of a coil spring. Design an experiment to investigate the effect of the bird's size on the number of oscillations of the spring. (When you stretch the spring to start the oscillations, be sure to stretch it to the same length each time.)

    What did you observe? Did the number of oscillations change with a bigger bird?

- Change the size of the coil spring. Keep the bird size constant. Stretch the spring to the same length each time.

    What effect did the new size have on the number of oscillations?

    Graph the size of the coil against the number of oscillations and make several predictions. Test your predictions.

Related activities: SS 2, SS 11

Color Me Purple, Blue, Green, Pink—Exploring the Colors in White Light

BIS **42**

Materials: piece of dark cardboard; mirror; shallow pan; glass container; water **More:** children's toy top; copy of disk patterns from page 61

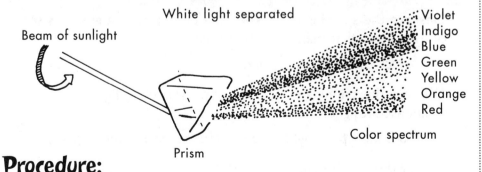

White light separated

Beam of sunlight

Prism

Color spectrum

Violet
Indigo
Blue
Green
Yellow
Orange
Red

Facts to know:

⬦ Sunlight is white light. When white light passes through a prism, it is separated into its component colors, the colors of the rainbow—red, orange, yellow, green-blue, indigo, and violet. Falling drops of water can act as a prism when light strikes them at the correct angle.

◇ ◇ ◇

Procedure:

- Cut a narrow slit about $\frac{1}{8}$ inch by 1 inch in the dark cardboard.

- Paste the slitted cardboard to a window through which sunlight streams into the classroom.

- Darken the other classroom windows.

- Fill a pan with water.

- Place a mirror against one edge of the pan. Let the sunlight that passes through the slit fall on both the water and the mirror. (Adjust the mirror as necessary so that a spectrum appears somewhere in the area underneath or beside the window.)

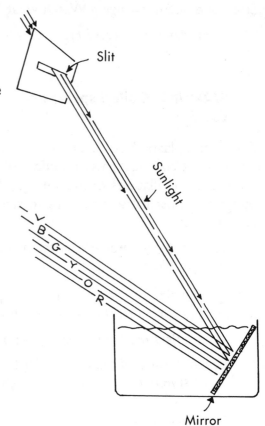

- Observe the spectrum. Record the order of the colors of the spectrum.

    Are these colors in the same order as the colors of a rainbow?

- Stir the water gently with your finger.

    What happens to the reflected spectrum?

- Next, let sunlight that has passed through the slit in the cardboard go through the glass container filled with water.

    What do you observe?

More:

- Use the disk patterns. Cut out the first disk. Poke a hole through the center.

- Place the disk on the flat area of the top. Spin the top as fast as you can.

- Observe the spinning disk. When the disk spins, the eye sees some of the colors that make up white light.

    Which colors do you observe?

- Observe the spinning disk in sunlight, fluorescent light, or incandescent light.

    Does the type of light have an effect on your observations?

- Repeat the activity with one of the other disk patterns.

    Does the new pattern make a difference? Explain.

Related activities: BIS 3, BIS 51, CSR 1, CSR 2, CSR 4

Colors can be created by combining and recombining colors. Red, yellow, and blue are called <u>basic</u>, or <u>primary</u>, <u>colors.</u> A combination of any two primary colors results in <u>secondary colors</u>. When primary and secondary colors are mixed, <u>tertiary colors</u> are formed. Yellow (primary) and green (secondary) can be mixed to form a yellow-green tertiary color.

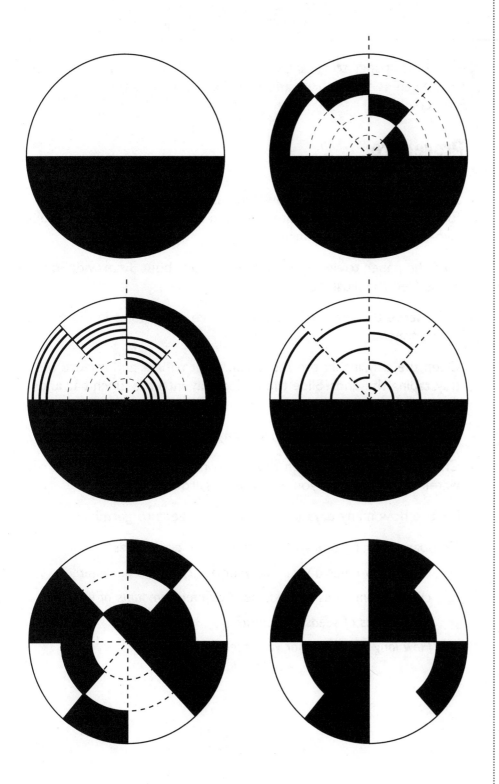

Lunch-Bag Garden—Studying Plant Growth

Materials: paper towel; paper lunch bag ($6\frac{1}{4}$ x $5\frac{1}{2}$ inches); vegetable seeds such as bean, corn, radish **More:** plant fertilizer; food coloring

Procedure:

- Fold a piece of the paper towel in half in one direction and then fold it in half in the opposite direction so that it will fit into about two-thirds of a paper lunch bag.

- Fold the paper towel again to make a tray about 3 cm wide for the seeds (see the illustration).

- To observe the roots of the plants, make small holes in the bottom of the tray.

- Open the tray, insert the seeds you want to use, and reclose the tray, taping the ends. Slide the folded tray into the lunch bag and dampen the tray with water.

- Place or hang your garden in a sunny place in the classroom.

- Check it daily. Water when the tray is dry. Record the amount of water and how often you water your garden.

- Record how many days it took for your seeds to germinate.

- Compare your results with those of your classmates.

    How many times a week did your plant need to be watered?

    Did different types of seeds need different amounts of water?

    What types of seeds grew best?

    How long did it take for your seeds to germinate?

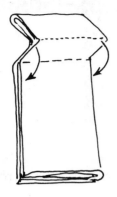
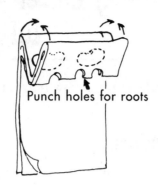

Punch holes for roots

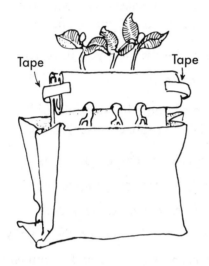

Tape   Tape

More:

- Water the plants in your garden with a solution of fertilizer and water.

    Did fertilizer really make a difference?

    Graph stem- and root-growth rates of the plants in relation to time. Compare your results with another classmate's results.

- Hang the gardens in the room on the north, south, east, and west walls, or on the outside of a building. Compare the growth rates.

    Was there a difference in growth rates? How can you explain it?

- Add food coloring to the water in your garden and observe what happens.

    What prediction can you make?

Related activities: BIS 2, BIS 21, BIS 24, BIS 78, SS 7

BIS 44

Every Litter Bit Helps—Science with Litter

Students will record and compare amounts and varieties of litter.

Materials: trash bag; magnet; string

Procedure:

- Collect some litter from your schoolyard and put it in the trash bag.

- When you return to your classroom, sort the litter into several piles; classify it by any method you wish.

- Have a friend guess the method you used to classify your litter.

    Was the guess correct?

- Count the number of items in each pile of litter and make a graph—bar graph, line graph, or histogram.

- Use your graph to answer these questions:

    How many kinds of litter did you find?

    Which type of litter was most common?

    Of which type of litter did you find the least? Why?

    What other inferences can you make from your graph?

- Try a different collection spot.

    Did you have the same results? Why were your results the same or different?

    How would the litter data you collected vary depending on whether you lived in a city like New York or in a small town?

    How would you compare these areas to a rural area or to your area?

- Draw a magnet tied to a string through your litter.

    Did you find a new way to classify your litter?

More:

- Prepare a list of suggestions for reducing the amount and type of litter you collected. Try your suggestions and then collect litter again.

    Did your suggestions work? Why or why not?

Related activities: BIS 26, BIS 63

Experimenting by Advertising— Analyzing Advertisements

> **Materials:** carpet advertisement that mentions scientific experiments conducted on carpet; carpet samples (wool and other fibers)

Procedure:

* Use the advertisement to identify experimental variables: type of product used to clean carpet; types of carpets (100% wool, wool blend, nylon, orlon); thickness of carpet pile; color of carpet; use of carpet (recreation room, kitchen, baby's room, living room); definition of clean.

* Develop your own experiments to test the hypothesis that a wool carpet can be cleaned more readily than carpets made from other fibers.

* Collect your data. Combine your data with other students and make a graph.

    Do you agree with the advertising claims? What would you state in your own ad?

    Is it important to examine for yourself the claims made in ads? Why?

    Where can you turn for help in investigating ad claims? What consumer groups can you name or find out about?

Adapted from Gerald H. Krockover, "Experiment Through Advertising," *Science and Children* (January/February 1973). pp. 28–29. By permission.

Related activities: BIS 39, BIS 53

BIS 46

Molecular Structure, or What Is This Stuff?

Materials: pint jar; cornstarch; water **More:** baking soda; salt; flour; other similar kitchen products

The molecular structure of the starch-water material maintains its structural integrity on impact, but under slow, steady pressure it will give easily.

Procedure:

* Add cornstarch to the jar until it is $\frac{1}{2}$ full.

* Add just enough water to make a thick paste. Slowly push your fingers directly into the paste.

* Now push your fingers rapidly into the paste.

    Was it harder to push your fingers rapidly into the paste?

    What explanations can you offer for this reaction?

    Is the cornstarch-water material a solid, liquid, or both? Explain your answer.

Related activities: BIS 34, BIS 39, BIS 53

BIS 47

Water–The Miracle Liquid

Materials: wax paper; toothpick; container; straight pin; soap or detergent; water **More:** rubbing alcohol; dropper; 3 toothpicks; soap or detergent

Students will experience various properties of water and conduct experiments to test their hypotheses.

The attraction (cohesiveness) of the water molecules for each other is greater than their attraction for the wax molecules on the wax paper.

Procedure:

* Sprinkle a few drops of water on the wax paper.

    Did the water spread out or form droplets?

* With the toothpick, break a drop into smaller and smaller drops.

    What shapes were the smaller drops?

    What does this tell you about the attraction of water molecules for each other?

* Float the straight pin in a glass with water. (If you have difficulty, place the pin on a piece of wax paper floating on the water, then gently push the paper away.)

* Drop a small chip of soap or detergent near the pin.

    What do you observe? Why does it happen?

66

Do you think that the soap changes the attraction of water molecules for each other? Why or why not?

More:

- Place the 2 toothpicks in water and touch the soaped tip of another toothpick between them. Now put a few drops of alcohol between the toothpicks.

    What do you observe at first? After the alcohol was added?

    What changed the surface tension?

- Design an activity to test this hypothesis: The smaller the diameter of a tube, the higher a liquid rises in the tube.

    Do your results confirm this hypothesis? Why or why not?

    What do you think caused the water to move up the tube?

Related activities: BIS 51, BIS 60

Facts to know:

- ◇ The attractive force of like molecules for each other is known as the <u>cohesive force.</u> This cohesiveness keeps like molecules together until the molecules meet another material.

- ◇ <u>Adhesion</u> makes unlike molecules attract each other more than like molecules.

◇◇◇

Make Your Deposit Here– Examining Sediments

BIS **48**

Materials: gallon jar; soil; clay; sand; gravel; pebbles; water **More:** filter paper; soda straw; metric balance

Students will observe, compare, and predict actions involved with the process of accumulating sediments.

Procedure:

- Put equal amounts of the soil, clay, sand, gravel, and pebbles into the gallon jar. Add enough water so that it is almost full.

- Carefully shake or stir the mixture thoroughly.

    Can you predict the order in which the materials will be deposited (settle out) in the jar?

- Stop stirring and let the mixture stand. Observe and record the order in which the materials settle out.

    Which material settles out first? Why? Last? Why?

    How well did your observations compare with your predictions?

    Would this be an accurate model for sediments settling on the sea floor?

    What is a list of variables that would control the rate at which sediments settle? Think about size of the particle, shape of the sediment, and density of the sediment.

    Can you design an investigation to show the effects of shape on the formation of sediments?

What if you use salt water instead of tap water or hot water instead of cool water? Will you get the same order and rate of settling for those sediments? Explain.

More:

* Weigh the piece of filter paper on a metric balance.

* After a 24-hour settling-out period, insert a soda straw into the gallon jug to collect samples of sediments still in solution.

* Cap the straw with your thumb to retain the water, remove the straw and water, and filter the solution through the filter paper. (The solid sediments are retained as the water passes through the filter paper.)

* Allow all the water in the filter paper to evaporate.

* Weigh the filter paper again. (The difference between the original weight of the filter paper and the weight with the sediment is the amount of sediment suspended in solution at the time and the level at which the sample was taken.)

* Take samples at various depths and time intervals.

* Record your data. Graph the results, plotting depth against time.

    Can you conclude anything from this graph about materials held in solution? Explain.

Related activities: BIS 15, BIS 17

BIS 49   Number of Turns, Number of Tacks

Materials: nail; thumbtacks; copper wire; three 1.5 volt batteries
More: cardboard; iron filings; insulated wire; battery

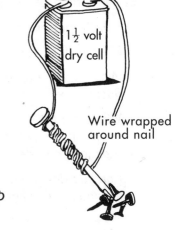

$1\frac{1}{2}$ volt dry cell

Wire wrapped around nail

WARNING: The wires and nails can get hot. Handle with care.

Procedure:

* Make an electromagnet by wrapping the wire around the nail and connecting the ends of the wire to the terminals of a battery.

* Use the electromagnet to pick up thumbtacks.

    How many thumbtacks can be picked up by your electromagnet?

What variables can you identify that will affect the strength of an electromagnet (measured by the number of thumbtacks picked up)?

- Vary the number of times the wire is wound around the nail (turns). Use the electromagnet to pick up tacks. Record the number of tacks picked up in each case.

- Prepare a data table comparing the number of turns with the number of tacks.

  Do your results indicate a trend?

  Do you notice that as the number of turns increases, the number of tacks picked up also increases up to a limit?

  How many tacks do you predict would be picked up by the electromagnet with four turns on the nail?

  What is the smallest number of turns that can be used to pick up the greatest number of tacks?

- Try the same activity using 2 and 3 batteries.

  Are the number of tacks picked up the same?

  Does it make any difference if you connect the batteries in parallel? In series?

  Predict the limit for a 4-battery system, using your results for a 1-, 2-, and 3-battery system.

More:

- Pass a length of wire through a hole in the cardboard. Connect the ends to the battery.

- Sprinkle some iron filings on the cardboard around the wire. Tap the cardboard gently with your finger.

  What do you observe?

- Thread a length of the wire through a sheet of cardboard to form a coil.

- Sprinkle some iron filings around the coil and connect the ends of the wire to the battery. Tap the cardboard gently with your finger.

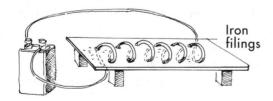
Iron filings

What do you observe? How can you explain your observations?

Related activity: SS 8

Facts to know:

◇ Batteries connected in parallel have one wire that connects similar terminals (for example, the negative terminals), and a separate wire joining all the remaining similar terminals (the positive terminals).

◇ Batteries connected in series have one wire going from the negative terminal of one battery to the positive terminal of another battery, and so on.

Overflowing Water—Mass, Volume, Displacement

Materials: 2-liter plastic container; hole punch; soda straw; modeling clay; rock; small plastic container; water **More:** string; rock; spring scale; metric balance

You can find the volume of an irregularly shaped object by putting it in a liquid. Measure the height of the liquid before and after the object is submerged. The difference between these two heights is a measurement of the volume of the object.

Procedure:

* Cut the top off the 2-liter container.

* Punch a hole in the wall of the container near the top.

* Insert the straw about 2 cm into this opening.

* Apply clay to seal the soda straw to the container.

* Place the small container below the straw spout to catch overflowing water.

* Determine the mass of this empty container.

* Fill the 2-liter container with water up to, but slightly below, the straw spout.

* Carefully immerse the rock in the water.

* Determine, in milliliters, the amount of the overflow.

   Why does water overflow when you add the rock? How can you determine the volume of the rock?

More:

* Attach a string to the rock.

* Weigh the rock with a spring scale, when suspended in air.

* Then submerge the rock in water in the container and weigh it again with the spring scale.

   How do these two weights compare?

* Collect the overflow water in the small plastic container.

* Determine the weight of the overflow (displaced water). (Remember to subtract the weight of the empty container from the weight of the small container plus the overflow water.)

   How does the weight of the displaced water compare with the weight of the rock when weighed in air and when weighed in water?

Related activities: BIS 20, BIS 23, BIS 30

Chromatography

Materials: filter paper, or paper towel, coffee filter, or tissues; glass jar with lid; pencil or soda straw; water-soluble black marker; scissors; water **More:** water-soluble markers—red, yellow, green, blue, orange, brown; filter paper; glass jar; pencil or straw; plastic pan; rubber band; rubbing alcohol; hole punch

Facts to know:

◇ <u>Chromatography</u> is a technique that separates a mixture into its individual parts.

◇◇◇

Procedure:

● Cut a 1-cm-wide strip of filter paper. The strip should be about 4 cm longer than the depth of the glass jar.

● Pour water into the jar to a depth of about 2 cm.

● Tape one end of the paper strip to the pencil or straw and wrap the strip around it several times.

● Use the water-soluble marker to make a heavy ink dot 4 cm above the bottom of the strip.

● Place the pencil or straw over the jar mouth and suspend the paper strip into the jar with the bottom of the strip touching the bottom of the jar. (The marker dot should be well above the water level in the jar.)

● Observe the paper every 5 minutes. (Different manufacturers of black markers use different components in their black ink. Results may vary from manufacturer to manufacturer. Try different brands until you get good color separation.)

When the water reaches the black marker dot, the various components (pigments) of black ink are separated. The pigments have differing masses and travel up the paper at different rates. The heaviest pigments separate out first and the lightest pigments separate out last, further up the paper.

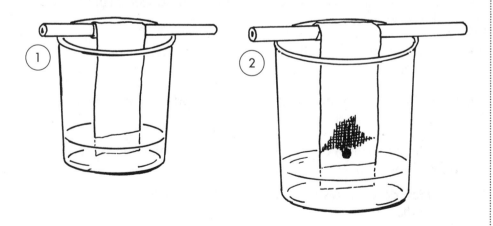

What happens to the black dot?

How does the water move up the paper?

What pigments are in the black marker dot?

More:

- Cut six 1-cm-wide strips of paper, 4 cm longer than the depth of the plastic pan.

- Stretch a rubber band across the plastic pan. Add water to the pan to a depth of 2 cm.

- Place a different-colored ink dot 4 cm from the bottom of each paper strip.

- Suspend the color-dotted strips from the rubber band so that they hang into the water. (All colored dots should be 2 cm above the water level.)

- Observe the paper strips every 5 minutes.

    Do all the color pigments rise at the same rate?

    Do different color dots take different amounts of time to separate? Make a graph of distance versus time. What kind of curve do you get?

    What pigments do you see in the trail formed by each separating color?

    Does each marker have its own characteristic fingerprint?

- Choose two colors of markers. Make a dot of one color on a strip of filter paper. Make a dot of the other color on top of the first color, being careful to leave no trace of the original colors.

- Trade strips with another student.

    How can you determine which colors are in the dot? Devise an experiment to find out.

    How can your results with the colored-dot separation help you find the answer?

- Cut a 1 cm strip of filter paper, about 4 cm longer than the depth of the glass jar.

- Place a dot of water-soluble black marker 2 cm from the bottom of the strip.

- Pour rubbing alcohol into the jar to a depth of 1 cm. Hang the paper from a pencil or straw as before.

- Cap the jar. (This lets the air inside the jar become saturated with alcohol vapors.)

    How do these results compare to the results when you used water in the jar?

- Cut a rectangle out of a sheet of filter paper. (When it is rolled into a cylinder, it should fit inside your jar.)

- Using a pencil, draw a baseline 2 cm from the bottom of the paper. This will be your reference line.

- Place a small pencil dot at 3-cm intervals along the baseline.

- Over each pencil dot, mark a dot from a different-colored marker.

- Beneath the dot, write the color's name in pencil. (The pencil marks will not be affected by the alcohol.)

- Form the rectangle into a cylinder.

- Place the cylinder into the jar containing alcohol up to a 1-cm depth. Cap the jar.

- Remove the paper before the alcohol reaches the top of the cylinder. (If it does reach the top, it will begin to move sideways and the colors will intermingle.)

- Allow the cylinder to dry.

    Do the individual colors all separate out the same?

    Do the individual colors travel up the paper at the same rate of speed?

    What color, if any, is most common in all the color separations?

- Punch a small hole in the center of a filter paper circle. Insert a small, rolled piece of filter paper through the hole in the center of the paper circle.

- Use colored markers to make concentric circles (one color for each concentric circle) on the paper circle.

- Place the assembly in the glass jar with alcohol. Cap the jar.

Describe your observations.

    How do these results compare to the results with the paper strips?

Related activities: BIS 47, BIS 89

Reducing Noise Pollution  BIS **52**

Materials: shoebox; scraps of paper, cardboard, wood, plastic, ceiling tile; alarm clock; meter stick; optional—decibel meter (speech and hearing teachers may have one)

Procedure:

- Place the alarm clock in the shoebox.

- Set the alarm and let it ring. Walk away from it until you can no longer hear the ringing. Measure the distance.

    How far away were you when you could not hear the sound?

* Now fill the shoebox with the paper scraps.

* Place the clock in the paper and measure the depth of the paper below and above the clock.

* As before, let the alarm ring and measure the distance at which you can no longer hear the ringing.

    How does this distance compare to the distance at which you heard the alarm before? Why is it different?

* Vary the material in the shoebox. Use cardboard, wood, and plastic. Repeat the activity with each of these materials.

* Record the distance from the shoebox where you couldn't hear the sound with each material.

* Arrange the materials from most effective sound absorber to the least effective sound absorber.

    Why do some materials reduce noise levels more than others?

    What contribution does distance from the sound source make?

    What if you put a sound source in a thermos? Could you hear it? Why or why not?

* If you can obtain a decibel meter, measure the decibel level of the alarm with each material in the box. Graph the decibel level for each material.

Related activities: BIS 26, BIS 44, BIS 63

BIS **53**

Paper Toweling—Which Is Best for You?

Materials: samples of 5 different brands of paper towel; embroidery hoop; 2 books; weights; quart jar; sandpaper; water
More: samples of different dishwashing detergents

Procedure:

* Use the data table to make a paper-towel ratings list. (The information available on the wrapper and your calculations complete the first 6 characteristics. You will be testing the remaining 6 qualities. Decide on a rating system for the data you collect, such as 1 to 10.)

* Stretch a sheet of toweling across an embroidery hoop to make it tight. Spread the hoop between two books.

	Towels per Roll	Square Feet per Roll	Plies per Sheet	Price per Roll	Unit Cost per 100 Towels	Unit Cost per 100 Square Feet	Wet Strength Rating	Dry Strength Rating	Water Absorption Rating	Tearing Ease	Abrasion Rating
Towel #1											
Towel #2											
Towel #3											
Towel #4											
Towel #5											

* Spray water across the toweling until it is saturated. With the paper toweling in this position, gently add weights until the toweling gives way.

* Record the weights necessary to tear the toweling. Repeat this process for each of the five samples of toweling.

    How could you test for dry strength? Try it. Repeat for all 5 samples.

* Pour 200 ml of water into the quart jar. Place a paper towel in the water.

* Remove it without squeezing it, but allow any runoff to drip back into the jar.

* Measure how much water is left in the jar. This is the amount of water absorbed by the sheet of paper towel. Record the amount in the table.

* Repeat for the other samples of toweling.

* Devise ways to test the tearing ease of the paper towels. (There are two different types of tearing. The tearing within a sheet of paper towel, and the tearing of sheets from the towel roll.

    How could you test the first type of tearing? Try it.

    How could you test the second type of tearing? Try it.

* Rub a sheet of paper towel across the sandpaper and observe the results.

* Repeat for all the brands of paper towel.

    Which paper towel had the highest rating? The lowest?

    Was the towel with the highest rating the best in all characteristics?

    If you wanted to scrub with a paper towel, which one would you choose? Why?

    If you wanted to clean up a water spill, which would you choose? Why?

The best performing towels are not necessarily the best buy for you. Sometimes a cheaper paper towel is preferred to the "best." It depends on what you want to use it for.

More:

* Devise a way to test which dishwashing detergent is best for you.

    What criteria will you select to test the dishwashing detergent of your choice? How will you test these criteria?

Related activities: BIS 39, BIS 45

How Does Your Light Dimmer Work?

Materials: light bulb; battery; 3 wires with alligator clips attached; piece of diffraction grating (obtained from commercial science suppliers); 20 to 30 cm tightly coiled narrow gauge spring; good conducting wire

Procedure:

* Darken the room. (If you cannot get total darkness, darken the room and then do the activity inside a large cardboard carton lying on its side with the top cut out.)

* Construct a closed circuit as shown in the diagram.

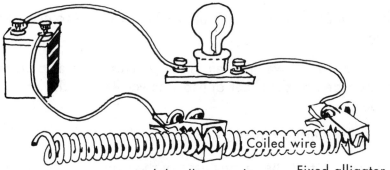

Mobile alligator clip   Fixed alligator clip

* Attach one alligator-clipped wire permanently to one end of the wire spring. Keep the other alligator-clipped wire in your hand.

* Touch the clip in your hand to the coiled spring near the permanently fixed clip. The bulb should light brightly.

* With the bulb lit, slide the clip down the length of the spring.

    What happens to the intensity of the burning bulb? What accounts for this?

    As you travel down the coiled wire spring, are you increasing or decreasing the amount of resistance to the electricity provided by the battery?

    Can you compare this process to a light dimmer? Can you use this comparison to explain how a light dimmer works?

- While the bulb is burning its brightest, observe the spectrum of the light through the diffraction grating.

- Continue observing the spectrum of the burning bulb while sliding the mobile wire down the spring.

    How does the spectrum change as you look at the bulb burning in these two instances?

- Observe the spectrum of the burning bulb again as you slide the mobile wire down the spring.

    What changes do you observe in the spectrum? Is the intensity of the component colors of the spectrum the same throughout?

    Relate the changes in temperature (burning intensity) of the bulb to the color shift in the spectrum when viewed through the diffraction grating.

    In the constellation Orion, three stars are distinctly visible: Betelgeuse (red), Sirius (white), and Rigel (blue). Which do you think is a hot star? A cold star? What evidence can you give to support your answer?

Related activity: SS 8

Can Soap Help?

BIS **55**

Materials: boat made from aluminum screen; liquid detergent; glass of water **More:** penny; dropper; water

Procedure:

- Float a screen boat in a glass of water.

- Add one drop of soap or detergent to the water.

    What do you observe? Can you explain the reaction?

More:

- Place a penny on a flat surface. Use the dropper to place drops of water on the penny.

    How many drops can stay on the penny? What keeps the drops on the penny?

    What does this tell you about the attraction of one water drop to another drop?

    Is the amount of drops the same for both sides of the penny?

Related activities: BIS 3, BIS 4

The surface tension of water is weakened by adding a small amount of soap or detergent. This is because the soap molecules move between the molecules of water, reducing the attraction of one molecule of water for another.

Mapping Elevations on Models

> **Materials:** clear plastic shoebox with clear lid; clay, wood, or plaster of Paris; grease pencil; metric ruler; water **More:** topographic map with at least 12 levels of elevation; cardboard; glue; scissors

Procedure:

* Make a model of a mountain from wood, plaster of Paris, or clay.

* Place the model in the clear plastic shoebox.

* Mark the side of the shoebox vertically into 1.5-cm intervals.

* Pour water into the container until it reaches the lowest mark.

* Put the lid on the container. (If you look into the container, you can see the outline formed by the water where it meets the model.)

* Use the grease pencil to trace this outline on the lid.

* Add water to the next mark and trace again. Continue adding water and tracing until you have reached the peak of your hill or mountain. (You now have a contour map on the box lid.)

    How can you tell if you are going down into a valley or up the mountain by observing the contour lines?

    If 1.5 cm = 100 m, what is the height of your mountain?

    How would a weather forecaster use a contour map? Does it measure the same things as your map of the mountain?

More:

* Select an 8 x 10-cm section from the topographic map.

* Cut out 12 pieces of cardboard, each measuring 8 x 10 cm. Following the major contour intervals, such as every 50 or 100 feet, cut out the map section representing the lowest elevation and glue it to a piece of cardboard.

* Cut the area representing the next highest elevation from the map, glue this piece on the second piece of cardboard, and trim the excess cardboard.

* Position and glue the second piece of cardboard on top of the first.

* Continue cutting and gluing sections of the map, in order of increasing elevation and along contours, until you have completed all sections. (You should end up with a three-dimensional model of the area shown on the map section.)

What geologic feature is represented by the topographic map you constructed?

Could you identify the structure before the model was made?

What geologic processes could have resulted in the formation of this feature?

Related activity: SS 17

Color and Light Mixing

Materials: 2-inch-diameter round button; red and green paint; paintbrush; string **More:** objects such as large square bead, cylinder, or pyramid

Procedure:

- Paint one side of the button in alternating segments of red and green.

- Thread a 60-cm piece of string through two of the buttonholes. Tie the ends of the string. Slide the button to the middle of the string.

- Hold the string in two hands, one on either side of the button.

- Twirl the string. Then let the string unwind as you push your hands closer together and farther apart. (This keeps the button spinning.)

    What do you observe about the colors on the button? Do they appear to change?

More:

- Try using another object instead of a button.

    Do you obtain the same results? Why or why not?

Related activities: BIS 31, BIS 59, BIS 88

Because of retinal retention, the mixing of red and green light is reflected to your eye as the color yellow. Blue and red would be seen as the color purple. Green and blue would be seen as peacock blue. Red, green, and blue would be seen as white.

Spacy Plants

Students will discover the relationship between plant growth and amount of space.

Materials: lima bean seeds; 2 plant pots of identical size; soil; small glass jar; plastic wrap; rubber band; paper towel; vermiculite; glass jar; water **More:** morning glory seeds; plant pot; stick

Procedure:

- Add soil to the pots.

- In one pot, plant 2 seeds. In the other pot, plant 10 to 15 seeds.

- Water the soil and put the pots where they will get some light.

- Observe the pots daily until the plants have sprouted and grown several leaves.

    What do you observe?

    Do plants need space to grow fully? Explain.

- Completely fill the jar with lima bean seeds. Add water to fill the jar to the top.

- Seal the jar with plastic wrap.

- Observe the beans after 24 hours.

- Describe your observations.

    Do plants exert pressure as they grow?

    Can you devise a technique to measure this force?

- Use the "Garden in a Jar" technique (BIS 2) to plant seeds.

- After the seeds have sprouted and rootlets, stems, and leaves are visible, turn the jar upside down.

- Observe what happens to the plant parts and their direction of growth.

    Can the growth of various plant parts be altered?

More:

- Plant and grow a morning glory plant in the pot.

- Place a stick in the pot.

- Observe the direction in which the stem winds itself around the stick.

    Is the growth direction of the stem clockwise or counterclockwise?

    Can the direction of a morning glory's growth be changed?

Related activities: BIS 2, BIS 21, BIS 24, BIS 43, BIS 78, SS 7

Through the Glass Rod—Observing and Analyzing

Materials: 10-cm glass rod, 4 to 5-mm thick; hollow glass rod; plastic rod; sheets of different kinds of paper with 4 words typed in uppercase—PUN, ART (in black), ECHO, BOX (in red) on each sheet

Procedure:

- Place the glass rod over the words on one kind of paper and then lift the rod slowly off the paper.

    What do you observe?

- Vary the type of paper, color of the words, and type of rod. (Be sure to type the words exactly as before.) In each case, place the rod over the words, lift the rod slowly off the paper, and observe the words.

    Does the paper make a difference?

    Does the rod make a difference?

    Does the color type make a difference?

    What do you observe about the words?

    Are they all uppercase? Does this offer an explanation?

    Reproduce the words in lowercase. What happens now?

Related activities: BIS 25, BIS 28, BIS 31, BIS 34

When you look through the rod, all the words are inverted. The black words look inverted. But the red words do not look inverted because of the shape of the letters in these words.

Do Aluminum Boats Float?

Materials: aluminum foil; plastic container; washers; metric balance; water   **More:** Styrofoam; wax paper; clay; soda pop; cooking oil; vinegar; syrup; water; pictures of various types of boats

Procedure:

- Make a shape out of aluminum foil that will float. Float it on water in a plastic container. (If your boat does not float, redesign it so that it will.)

    What are the dimensions of your aluminum boat?

    How much does it weigh?

    What did you have to consider when you made the boat?

- Using washers as weights, find out how many weights your boat will support before it sinks.

- Weigh your aluminum boat with the weights required to sink it. Find how many weights equal the weight of your boat.

- Compare your results with those of your classmates.

    Whose boat held the most weight? Did everyone begin with the same-size boat?

More:

- Conduct an aluminum-boat contest.

    Who can make the biggest boat? The smallest?

    Which boat supports the most sinkers?

    Who can construct the longest boat that will float?

    Can you keep your boat afloat with a hole in it?

    Can it float with a hole above the waterline? A hole below the waterline?

- Make same-size boats out of Styrofoam, wax paper, and clay.

    Which material will support the most weights?

- Float your boats in cold, lukewarm, and hot water. Try different liquids in the container—soda pop, cooking oil, vinegar, and syrup. Try to float all your boats in each liquid.

    Does the temperature of the water make a difference?

    Does the liquid make a difference? How does your aluminum boat float in soda pop, cooking oil, vinegar, or syrup?

- Examine pictures of various types of boats— steamboats, rafts, canoes, sailboats, and rowboats.

    Why are they shaped as they are?

Related activities: BIS 37, BIS 77, BIS 79, BIS 80

BIS **61**

Interpreting Data

Materials: Copy of graph (see page 83)

Procedure:

- The graph on page 83 is made from data on a test plot of grass that had dandelions growing on it. The data were collected over two years and are based on the number of dandelions counted in the test plot each month for 25 months.

What trend or trends do you notice?

What is the average number of months between the maximum numbers of dandelions counted? Which months are these?

How many dandelions do you expect in June 2001? December 2001? June 2002? August 2003?

In what month do you expect the next maximum number of dandelions to be counted?

Can you identify at least four variables that might have affected the data presented in this dandelion graph?

Where in the continental United States is this grass plot, north or south, east or west?

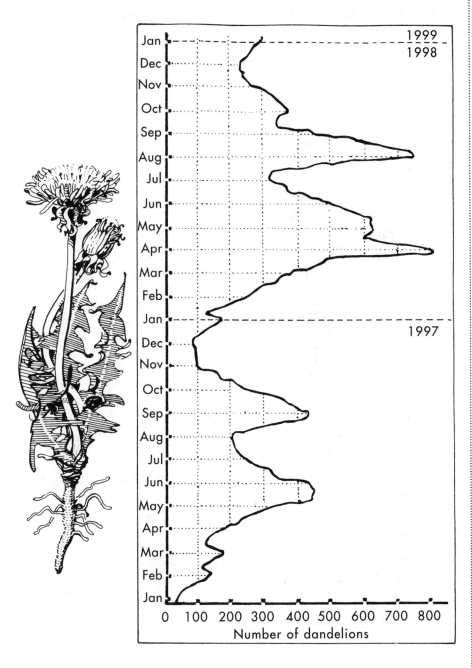

Related activities: BIS 9, BIS 15, BIS 32, BIS 35, BIS 39

Now You See It, Now You Don't

Students engage a discrepant event and analyze their observations to explain the event.

Materials: three 1-foot lengths of flexible tubing; glass Y or T; string; 2 balloons of similar size and shape; 2 clothespins **More:** thick felt marker; balloons; empty milk carton; stapler; scissors; section of rain gutter capped and sealed at both ends

Procedure:

- Attach flexible tubing to all three ends of a glass T (or Y). Tie string around the connections to make them tight.

- Attach balloons to any two ends of the tubing.

- Blow through the other piece of tubing to inflate the balloons. Blow one balloon twice the size of the other.

- Pinch off the tubes with clothespins so that no air escapes.

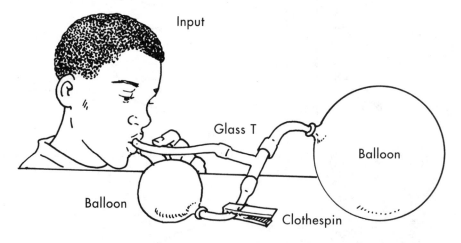

Input
Glass T
Balloon
Balloon
Clothespin

What do you think will happen when you open the passageway, allowing the free flow of air from one balloon to the other (the input tubing must still remain pinched off)?

Will the larger balloon become larger and the smaller balloon become smaller?

Will the smaller balloon become larger and the larger balloon become smaller?

Will the air distribute itself equally? Will the two balloons end up the same size?

Is it easier to blow up a new balloon or an old balloon? How does the answer to this question help you find the explanation?

More:

- Using a thick felt marker, draw various geometric shapes, such as circles, triangles, and squares, on an uninflated balloon.

    What will the shapes look like when the balloon is inflated?

    Will the geometric shapes look the same? Larger? Distorted?

- Lay an empty milk carton on its side. Staple the spout end closed, and cut out the top portion. (You now have a boat.)

- Blow up a balloon and pinch the end closed. Stuff the balloon inside the milk carton.

- Place the milk-carton boat in a rain gutter filled with water. Release your fingers from the pinched end of the balloon and let the boat go.

- Measure, record, and graph your results.

    How far did it travel? What variables affect its motion? Who can make it go the greatest distance?

Related activities: BIS 42, BIS 65, BIS 67

Soda Straw Symphony BIS 63

Materials: soda straw

Procedure:

- Flatten one end of a soda straw about $\frac{3}{4}$ inch of the way along the straw.

- Clip off the corners on the flattened end.

- Place the cut end in your mouth so that the corners do not touch your lips.

- Blow hard. (You should be able to make a low-pitched sound.)

- Keep blowing as you cut off short lengths of straw.

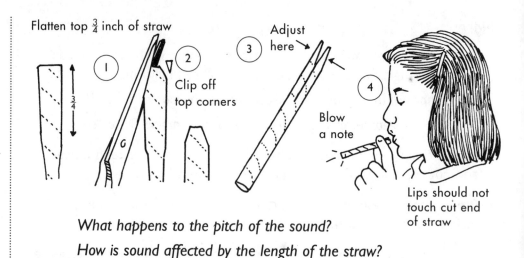

Flatten top ¾ inch of straw

Clip off top corners

Adjust here

Blow a note

Lips should not touch cut end of straw

What happens to the pitch of the sound?

How is sound affected by the length of the straw?

Related activities: BIS 13

A Day in the Sun

Materials: pencil; book; sheet of lined paper; tape

WARNING: Never look directly at the sun.

Procedure:

- Tape the pencil across the book.

- Place the book on the sheet of lined paper, aligning the lines so that they are parallel to the pencil.

- Place this assembly in direct sunlight, pointing the long axis of the book toward the sun.

- Mark the end of the shadow on the paper, on the line nearest to the shadow.

- Mark the length of the shadow every hour.

  What happens to the length of the shadow?

  How do the shadows change?

  What kind of shadow pattern will you get if you turn the assembly each hour, pointing it directly at the sun? Will the shadows vary?

  Will you get different results if shadow recordings are taken in different seasons? Explain.

Related activities: BIS 38, BIS 85

Students construct, observe, and record data to explain changes in the movement of the sun.

Facts to know:

◇ The sun makes an arc as it appears to move through the sky from east to west.

◇ ◇ ◇

In the Northern Hemisphere, the sun appears to rise higher in the summer months than in the winter months.

The Obedient Can, or the Elastic Motor

Materials: coffee can with plastic lid; rubber bands of different sizes; washers; 2 kitchen matches with heads broken off; nail; hammer; file **More:** rubber band; coffee can; washer

Procedure:

- Use the nail and hammer to punch a hole in the center of the bottom of the coffee can and in the center of the plastic lid.

- Smooth the holes with a file.

- Thread the rubber band through the hole in the bottom of the can.

- Insert a match through the rubber band at the bottom of the can.

- Attach 10 washers to the rubber band.

- Pull the remaining end of the rubber band through the opening in the cover. Keep this end in place with the other match.

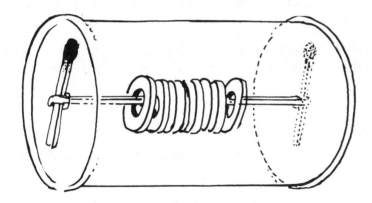

- Close the can.

- Roll it on the floor.

- Just before it stops, tell it to return to you.

    What do you observe? Can you explain why this happens?

- Repeat the activity with a different-size rubber band, with the washers in a different location, and with a different number of washers. In each case roll the can and observe what happens.

    Does it make a difference when you use a different size rubber band?

    What difference does it make when you relocated the washers?

    What difference does increasing or decreasing the washers make?

Students construct a mobile device and manipulate variables, record data, and assemble graphs to explain changes in motion.

The washers on the rubber band cause the rubber band to twist when the can is pushed. The harder the initial push, the more the rubber band will wind. When the energy given by the initial push is used up, the can will stop. The accumulated energy in the twisted rubber band makes it unwind, and the can rolls back.

Would the surface that the can is rolled on change the movement of the can?

Would the size of the can change the movement of the can?

More:

- Punch another hole in the bottom of the coffee can and another hole in the plastic lid.

- Thread the rubber band through all four holes in a figure 8.

- Tie the rubber band ends together.

- Fasten the washer to the center of the rubber band, where it crosses inside the can.

- Roll the can away from you.

    How does the action of this can compare with the original design?

Related activities: BIS 34, BIS 42, BIS 49, BIS 55, BIS 79

BIS **66**

Who Stole Our Peanut Brittle? An Investigation about Fingerprinting

Materials: stamp pad; paper; copy of "Who did it?" p. 89; **More:** nylon stocking; embroidery hoop; powdered sugar; ruler; raindrops

Procedure:

- Ink your right thumb on the stamp pad. Press and roll your thumb on paper.

- Repeat for the other fingers on your right hand. (If the fingerprint smudges or is blurry, repeat until you get clear prints.)

- Write down four observations about your fingerprints. Identify which print came from your thumb and from your middle finger.

    Do your fingerprints look like arches, loops, or whorls?

    Can a classmate identify which print is your thumb and which print is your middle finger?

- Two pieces of peanut brittle have been stolen from the box. Two right-hand thumbprints are found on the box and are shown on your handout.

- Write down at least 10 observations you can make about the fingerprints. Then compare the fingerprints found on the box to the fingerprints of the five people shown on your handout.

Does it help to measure any of the fingerprints?

Can you find three ways of classifying them?

Which print does your thumbprint resemble most?

Can you identify the person who stole the peanut brittle?

More:

- Tightly stretch one layer of the nylon stocking across an embroidery hoop.

- Dust it with a thin layer of powdered sugar.

- Collect some raindrops. (As the raindrops strike the surface they will pass through the nylon, dissolving the powdered sugar. This will leave dark spots—the raindrop prints.)

- Measure the size of the spots with a ruler.

What do you observe?

The three forms of fingerprints:

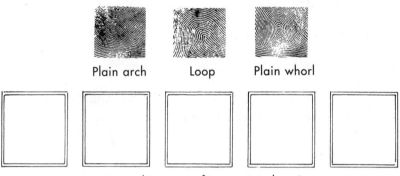

Plain arch   Loop   Plain whorl

Try making your fingerprints here!

Who stole our peanut brittle?

These are the two right-hand thumbprints we found on the peanut brittle box.

Wayne   Lynn   Kathy   Joe   Carol

Who did it?

Related activities: BIS 1, BIS 8, BIS 18, BIS 42, SS 10

Musical Sounds–Investigating with Sound

Materials: small fruit can with both ends removed; piece of balloon; piece of pocket mirror; glue; rubber band; flashlight **More:** rubber bands of different length and thickness; shoebox

Facts to know:

◇ Sounds are made by vibrating objects.

◇ The <u>amplitude</u> of a sound wave is an indication of how much energy was used to produce it. The greater the amplitude, the greater the volume.

◇ <u>Frequency</u> is the number of vibrations, or waves, in a specific time. The faster the object vibrates, the higher the pitch.

◇◇◇

WARNING: Handle the mirror carefully. The edges may be sharp.

Procedure:

- Tightly stretch the balloon piece over one end of the fruit can. Secure it with the rubber band.

- Glue the piece of mirror to the balloon, slightly off-center.

- Darken the classroom.

- Move the can near the chalkboard.

- Hold it away from and at an angle to the chalkboard.

- Shine the beam of a flashlight so that it strikes the mirror and bounces onto the chalkboard. (See the illustration.)

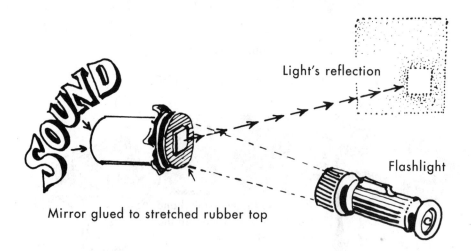

Light's reflection

Flashlight

Mirror glued to stretched rubber top

- Speak, sing, shout, or blow a whistle into the can.

- Observe the reflection cast on the blackboard.

- Describe your observation.

   How can the reflection be changed?

   Does singing vowels loudly in succession change the reflection? What about consonants?

   How does the reflection vary in relation to the strength of sound used?

More:

- Stretch a rubber band across the width of the shoebox. Then pluck it and listen to the sound.

- Vary the length of the rubber band by stretching it across the length of the shoebox. Pluck it and listen to the sound.

- Then repeat the activity with rubber bands of different length and thickness.

  How does the vibration of a rubber band vary as its length does?

  How will the pitch change as length does?

  Does the vibration depend on the diameter of the rubber band?

  Does the vibration rate depend on its tension?

Related activities: BIS 14, BIS 83, SS 14

Rising Raisins—Changes in Density   BIS 68

Materials: drinking glass; carbonated beverages; raisins; metric scale
More: baking soda; vinegar; drinking glass

Procedure:

- Fill the glass with a carbonated drink.

- Place 6 to 10 raisins in the glass.

  What do you observe?

  What causes the raisins to rise and sink?

  Will the raisins respond in the same way in tap water? What might be responsible for this action?

- Try several other carbonated drinks.

  Which gives you the best results?

  How do the raisins differ when at the bottom and at the top?

  How frequently does one raisin rise and sink? How long does it take to make the round trip?

- Repeat the activity, but weigh the raisins before putting them into the liquid. Notice the lightest and heaviest.

  Does the mass affect the frequency of the rising and falling raisin cycle?

More:

* Place some baking soda in the bottom of the glass. Add water until it is $\frac{3}{4}$ full. Slowly add vinegar.

* Add 6 to 10 raisins.

    What do you observe?

    Does this change the raisin cycle? Explain.

Related activities: BIS 33, BIS 40

BIS 69

The Egg In and Out of the Bottle— Experimenting with Air Pressure

Materials: I hard-boiled egg, shelled (the egg should be slightly larger than the mouth of the bottle); glass bottle; matches

Procedure:

* Wet the egg and the mouth of the bottle.

* Drop a burning match into the bottle.

* Quickly place the egg, pointed end down, into the mouth of the bottle.

    What happens? Can you explain why?

* Leave the egg inside the bottle. Rinse the bottle to remove the burned match and other debris.

* Tilt your head back. Hold the bottle vertical, with the pointed end of the egg in the mouth of the bottle.

* Place your finger around the mouth of the bottle and blow as hard as you can.

* As you blow, point the bottle toward a wastebasket. (The egg exits quickly.)

    How can you explain what happens?

When the flame goes out, the air inside the bottle cools and contracts, forming a vacuum. The air pressure inside the bottle is less than the air pressure outside the bottle. So, the egg is drawn inside the bottle.

Related activities: BIS 12, BIS 20, BIS 30, BIS 50

Starchy Science—Testing for Starch

Materials: iodine solution; dropper; containers; glass jar; spoon; starch powder; potato slice; bread; cooked rice; butter; sugar; cornflakes; water **More:** broad-leaf plant; aluminum foil; paper clips; ethyl alcohol; iodine solution

WARNING: Iodine is a poison. Do NOT eat any food on which you have placed iodine.

Procedure:

* Stir a bit of starch powder into a small amount of water in the glass jar. Add a few drops of iodine solution.

   What change do you observe?

   What inferences can you make?

* Predict the results if you add iodine to containers with a potato slice, a piece of bread, a slice of apple, a spoonful of cooked rice, butter, sugar, cornflakes.

* Record your predictions and then do the iodine test.

   Are your predictions confirmed by the results?

   Does the percentage of starch in a food make a difference in testing for starch?

More:

* Cut a strip of aluminum foil to fit across one plant leaf. The strip should be about $\frac{1}{2}$ to $\frac{3}{4}$ inch wide.

* Stretch the strip across the leaf and paper clip it at both ends.

* Place the plant in sunlight with the foil strip on the leaf.

* After 2 days, remove the leaf from the plant.

* Take off the foil and soak the leaf in ethyl alcohol for a few hours.

* Place a few drops of iodine both on the area previously covered by the strip and on areas not covered by the strip.

   Which area lacks starch?

   Do plants need sunlight to make starch? Why?

Related activity: BIS 62

Facts to know:

◇ Starch is made by plants and animals as a way to store sugar. A starch molecule is a long chain of sugar molecules.

◇ ◇ ◇

A simple test for starch is the iodine test. A few drops of iodine are placed on food. If starch is present, the iodine changes from reddish-brown to blue-black.

Exploring Concepts: Mass, Volume, and Displacement

BIS **71**

Materials: 3 baby food jars with lids; 3 peanut butter jars with lids; three 1-qt mayonnaise jars with lids; graduated cylinder; unpopped popcorn; marbles; BBs **More:** popped corn; container of known volume; cotton balls; water glass; water

Procedure:

* Assemble 3 sets of jars, each set with 1 baby food jar, 1 peanut butter jar, and 1 mayonnaise jar.

* Use the graduated cylinder to determine the volume of each jar.

* Fill all jars of the first set with marbles; the second with popcorn kernels; the third with BBs.

* Count the number of kernels, marbles, and BBs in the baby food jars. Record these numbers.

    Can you estimate the number of kernels in the peanut butter jar? In the mayonnaise jar?

    Can you estimate the number of marbles in the peanut butter jar? In the mayonnaise jar?

    Can you estimate the number of BBs in the peanut butter jar? In the mayonnaise jar?

* Now count the number of each item in each jar.

    Are your estimates correct?

    Does three times as much of something need three times as much volume?

* Observe the nesting of the popcorn kernels, marbles, and BBs in the smaller jars of all three sets.

    Which item has the greatest amount of space between each piece?

    If you combine the marbles and the BBs together, will you double the volume? (Combine the marbles and BBs together, and find out if your prediction was correct.)

More:

* Fill a container of known volume with the popped corn. Count the pieces of popped corn.

    How much unpopped corn would it take to make this much popped corn? What is the ratio of the unpopped-corn volume to the popped-corn volume?

94

- Fill a glass to the very top with water. (Be careful not to let the water spill. If the outside of the glass gets wet, the results are affected.)

- Make a prediction about whether or not you can get anything else into the glass without spilling the water.

- Slowly add cotton puffs. Keep adding them.

    What do you observe? Why does it happen?

    Where do the cotton fibers fit?

    Do you think water molecules have pore spaces between them?

Related activities: BIS 23, BIS 33, BIS 34

Balloon-ology–Exploring Properties of Air

Materials: two 125-ml Pyrex Erlenmeyer flasks; 2 balloons of equal size and shape (must fit snugly over the mouths of the flasks); heat source; clamp; ring stand; water **More:** 2-hole rubber stopper; bottle; 2 plastic drinking straws; balloon; 3 cylindrical shaped balloons; fishing line; 3 drinking straws; tape; felt-tip pen; beeswax

WARNING: This activity should only be done under the direct supervision of the teacher. Be careful. The flask will be hot.

Procedure:

- Place 10 ml of water in each flask.

- Stretch the mouth of 1 balloon over the mouth of 1 flask.

- Place this flask over a heat source. Bring the water to a boil. (The balloon will inflate.)

- Allow the flask to cool. (Place the flask under cold running tap water to cool it quickly.)

    What do you observe about the balloon?

- Next, bring the water to a boil in the second flask. Let it boil for several minutes, but leave about 1 to 2 ml of water in the flask.

- Quickly cap the flask with the other balloon. BE CAREFUL since the flask is very hot.

Air expands when heated. Capping the flask makes a closed system, trapping air. When the system cools, the air contracts. If the flask is capped <u>before</u> heating, the balloon inflates when heated and deflates when cooled. When the flask is capped <u>after</u> heating, heated expanded air escapes and a reduced amount of air is trapped. The disequilibrium or imbalance causes the balloon to go into the flask and inflate inside out.

- Place the flask back on the heat source. Heat the water to boiling.

   What do you observe about the balloon?

- Turn off the heat source and cool the flask under cool tap water.

- As the balloon deflates, guide it into the flask.

   Does the balloon inflate in the flask? Why does the balloon inflate inside out?

   Why does one balloon deflate while the other does not?

More:

- Seal the bottle with the stopper. Insert 2 straws through the holes in the stopper. (You may need to lubricate the straws to make them slide in easily.)

- Make sure the straws fit tightly in the stopper. (The straws should fill the holes with no gaps for air to leak through.)

- Attach a balloon to one of the straws and secure it tightly.

- Suck in on the other straw.

   What do you observe?

   How can you explain your observations?

   Can you inflate one balloon inside another balloon?

- Print your name on a deflated balloon with the felt-tip pen.

- Inflate it.

   What happens to the size of the printing as you inflate the balloon?

- Cut 3 lengths of fishing line the length of the classroom.

- Thread one fishing line through each of the 3 straws. (The straw should be able to slide up and down the string.)

- Keep the line taut and attach each end to a chair. (See illustration.)

- Inflate 3 cylindrical balloons to equal volumes.

- Use tape to attach an inflated balloon to the straws.

- Release the air from the balloon to propel the balloon as far down the string as possible.

- Repeat with the other 2 balloons.

- Rub the string with beeswax. Repeat the activity.

- Try a different-shaped balloon. Repeat.

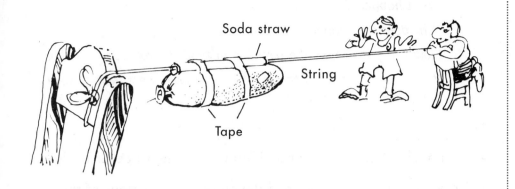

Which balloon traveled the farthest?

Does rubbing the string with beeswax make a difference?

Does a different balloon shape make a difference?

Will inclining or declining the string make a difference?

Related activities: BIS 41, BIS 65, BIS 67

The Rotating Propeller

BIS **73**

Materials: 6-inch length of $\frac{1}{4}$-inch dowel; 10-inch length of $\frac{3}{8}$-inch dowel (with grooves cut along one side $\frac{1}{2}$-inch apart and $\frac{1}{8}$-inch deep); 2-inch rectangle of thick plastic (with hole in center); nail (smaller than the diameter of the hole in the plastic); hammer
More: colored nail polish

Procedure:

- Use the nail to attach the plastic rectangle to one end of the long dowel. (This is the propeller.)

- Move the small dowel up and down the long dowel at right angles to the grooves.

The propeller enables students to manipulate variables to explain changes in the speed and direction of motion.

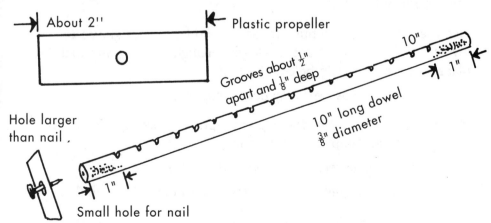

What happens?

Why does the propeller rotate?

How can you reverse the direction of propeller rotation?

What would happen if the number of grooves were increased, or the grooves were deeper?

More:

- Paint a dot of colored nail polish on one of the propeller blades.

- Stroke the grooves and record the number of rotations of the blade.

  Does the propeller change speed when the stroking is increased? How fast does it go?

Related activities: BIS 37, BIS 60, BIS 77, BIS 79

BIS 74

Boiling Water by Cooling

Materials: 250 or 500 ml Pyrex boiling flask; tight-fitting greased stopper; ring stand; burette clamp; heatproof gloves; heat source; catch basin; water

Boiling continues as long as there is a difference in temperature between the water that remains in the flask and the air temperature.

WARNING: This activity should only be done under the direct supervision of the teacher. The water contained in the flask is extremely hot. A poorly fitted stopper could cause leakage or burns.

Procedure:

- Pour water into the flask until it is half full. Place the flask on the ring stand, and heat the water to boiling.

- Let the water boil for several minutes.

- Shut off the heat. One minute later, press the greased stopper into the mouth of the flask.

- Use the ring stand, the burette clamp, and heatproof gloves to invert the flask. Place it upside down through the ring and lock into place. Put a catch basin below the flask.

  What do you observe? Why does it happen?

- When the boiling slows down, place a piece of wet cloth over the top of the flask. Keep the cloth moist.

  What do you observe? Can you explain why?

  What does the wet cloth do to the flask? To the air in the flask?

Related activities: BIS 33, BIS 34, BIS 69

Soil Testing

> **Materials:** *Part One:* thermometer; meter stick
>
> *Part Two:* 2 soil samples (coarse sand, clay); filter paper; 2 coffee cans with both ends removed; rubber bands; screen; 2 wide mouth jars; oven; water
>
> *Part Three:* 2 soil samples (coarse sand, clay); 2 tuna fish cans; rubber bands; knife; heat-resistant jar; oven; water
>
> *Part Four:* 4 or more soil samples; 8 paper cups; baking soda; lime; vinegar; lemon juice; water; red and blue litmus paper

PART ONE: SOIL TEMPERATURE _____

Procedure:

* Select a sunny spot outdoors. Record the air temperature.

* Record the soil temperature at the soil surface and at depths of 5, 10, 15, and 20 cm.

* Repeat this procedure in a shady spot; on a north-facing hill; a south-facing hill; and in wet, dry, and damp soil. Record the soil temperatures in all these locations.

  > *How do the temperatures of the soil and air compare? What is the relationship between soil temperature and soil depth?*
  >
  > *Which type of soil shows the greatest temperature variation? The least temperature variation?*
  >
  > *What is the relationship between the moisture content and the soil temperature?*

PART TWO: SOIL MOISTURE _____

Procedure:

* Attach a piece of filter paper to the base of each of the coffee cans with the rubber bands.

* Collect equal amounts of 2 different soil samples in the cans.

* Dry the soil samples in an oven set at 100° C (212° F) for 24 hours.

* Place each can on a screen above a jar. Pour equal amounts of water into each can.

- Measure the time it takes for the water to begin dripping into each jar, how long the water continues to drip into each jar, and how much water passes through each soil type.

- Prepare a graph of your data.

  Why do some soil samples absorb large amounts of water while others cannot?

  Which soil sample absorbs the most water?

  How could you determine which soil absorbs water the fastest?

  What are the advantages and disadvantages of fast water absorbtion by the soil?

PART THREE: SOIL PORE SPACE

Procedure:

- Oven dry 2 soil samples for 24 hours at 100° C. Measure the internal diameter and height of a tuna fish can. Attach filter paper to one end with a rubber band.

- Place a second rubber band on the other end of the can.

- Weigh the can and filter paper. Record the mass.

- Wet the filter paper and reweigh. Record the mass.

- Add 8 to 10 g of soil at a time to the can. Settle the soil by tapping the top of the can after each addition.

- When the can is full, level off the top and tap the can. Continue to add soil until only a very slight settling occurs. Level the top of the can.

- Place the can in 1 to 2 cm of water overnight. (In the morning, a portion of soil will have expanded above the top of the can.)

- Remove the soil that is above the top of the can with a knife blade drawn across the top of the can.

- Weigh the can with the remaining wet soil. Record the mass.

- Dry the soil in the can for 24 hours at 100° C.

- Cool the can and its contents. Weigh and record the mass.

- Repeat these steps with the second soil type.

- Use the following formula to calculate the percentage of pore space in the soil sample:

$$\text{Percentage of pore space} = \frac{\text{Mass of wet soil} - \text{mass of dry soil}}{\text{Internal volume of can}} \times 100$$

Here are some formulas to help:

Mass of wet soil = (mass of can + wet paper + wet soil) − (mass of can + wet paper)

Mass of dry soil = (mass of can + dry paper + dry soil) − (mass of can + dry paper)

Internal volume of can = π (internal diameter of can/2)^2 x height of can

> *Which soil type has the largest percentage of pore space?*
>
> *Infer why air is necessary in soil.*
>
> *How might water be drawn from pore spaces under normal conditions?*
>
> *How might rainstorms or changes in the atmospheric pressure bring fresh air into the soil?*

PART FOUR: CHEMICAL SOIL TESTS _____

Procedure:

* Into each of 4 paper cups, add $\frac{1}{2}$ cup of water.

* Add a teaspoon of baking soda to one cup, a teaspoon of lime to the second cup (both alkaline); a teaspoon of vinegar to the third cup, and a teaspoon of lemon juice to the fourth cup (both acid).

* Dip blue litmus paper in each cup, using a separate strip for each.

> *What color change do you observe when the paper is moistened with an acid? With an alkaline?*

* Repeat with strips of red litmus paper.

> *What do you observe? What color change do you see with an acid? With an alkaline?*

* Put a teaspoon of each soil sample into separate cups. Add $\frac{1}{2}$ cup of water to each and stir.

* After the soil has settled, test it with blue and red litmus paper.

> *Which soils are alkaline? Which are acidic? Which are neutral (no color change on the litmus paper)?*

* Take an acidic soil. (If you have none, add a teaspoon of vinegar to a neutral or alkaline soil.) Add a pinch of lime and stir. Test it with litmus paper.

> *Have you changed the soil to alkaline?*
>
> *Why do you think a farmer adds lime to his soil?*
>
> *Why are different fertilizers used for different purposes?*
>
> *Prepare a chart showing the compositions of different fertilizers and their uses.*

Related activities: BIS 2, BIS 24, BIS 78, SS 7

You Turned the Tables on Me–Investigating Rotation

Materials: turntable; cardboard circle cut to fit turntable; 2 pencils **More:** globe that spins; chalk

Procedure:

- Place the cardboard circle on the turntable and make it spin. (If the cardboard doesn't spin, tape it down to the turntable.)

- With the turntable spinning, try to draw a straight line on the cardboard with a pencil.

    What do you observe? Why does it happen?

- Try to draw a circle on the cardboard without moving the tip of your pencil.

- Now try using two pencils at once to draw a small circle and a large circle at the same time without moving either pencil.

- Compare the length of time it took to draw the two circles.

- Under which pencil is the turntable moving faster?

- Try changing the speed of the pencil as you move it across the cardboard.

    What patterns do you observe as the movement of the pencil changes?

    What will your line look like if you move your pencil from the outer edge of the spinning cardboard to the center? Test your prediction.

More:

- Have a partner rotate a globe counterclockwise. Place your chalk on the equator and try to draw a straight line toward the North Pole.

- Record your observations.

- Try again, this time move toward the South Pole.

    What do you observe?

    How does this relate to the turntable activity?

    How do your chalk lines relate to an air mass moving northward from the equator or a rocket ship launched northward?

Related activities: BIS 42, BIS 50

The Paper Whirlybird—More about Rotation

Materials: $8\frac{1}{2}$ x 11-inch paper; scissors; copy of whirlybird instructions

Procedure:

- Cut an $8\frac{1}{2}$ x 2-inch strip of paper. Gently tear one end of the strip down the middle about $\frac{1}{3}$ of the length of the paper.

- About $\frac{1}{2}$ inch above the end of the tear, make two tears, one from each side, about $\frac{1}{3}$ the width of the paper.

- Fold each torn section toward the middle, forming a 3-fold shank.

- Fold the bottom of the shank up about 1 inch to form a stem.

- Fold, but do not crease, the other end of the paper to make 2 wings.

- Throw the whirlybird up into the air as high as you can.

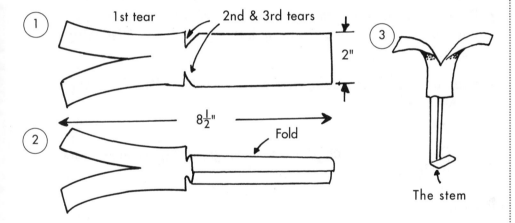

- Observe and describe the descent.

    Do the blades rotate clockwise or counterclockwise?

    What influences the direction of rotation?

    What is the rate of descent?

Related activities: BIS 37, BIS 60, BIS 73, BIS 79

Jack and the Beanstalk—Growing Plants from Plant Parts

Materials: root vegetables with tops (carrot, beet, turnip, sweet potato); shallow dish; pebbles; 2 avocado pits; 2 drinking glasses; 6 toothpicks; water **More:** seeds from fruit (peach, apple, apricot, pear); nuts (walnut, almond); planting pots; soil

Procedure:

- Cut 1 inch or 2 inches from the top of one of the root vegetables.

- Place the piece with its top in a shallow dish filled with pebbles. Add enough water to cover most of the bottom part of the piece.

- Place the dish in a sunny window and water as needed.

- Observe daily.

    What do you observe? Can you explain why it happens?

- Remove the hard coat from 2 avocado pits. Insert three toothpicks into each pit to keep part of it above water.

- Put one pit, pointed end down into a glass nearly filled with water. Put the other pit, pointed end up into a glass nearly filled with water.

- Keep both pits and glasses in the dark for 3 weeks until roots appear.

    What do you observe?

    Does the orientation of the pit affect growth? (pointed end versus nonpointed end up)

More:

- Store seeds in the refrigerator at 40° F. Provide moisture by placing the seeds in plastic bags with wet vermiculite. The length of chilling time needed is listed below:

Almonds	4 weeks	Peaches	3 months
Apples	2–3 months	Pears	2–3 months
Apricots	3–4 weeks	Walnuts	3 months
Grapes	3 months	Grapefruits	none

- Plant walnuts about 4–6 inches deep and all the others about 3 inches deep.

    Why do you think seeds of deciduous fruits and nuts need a period of moist chilling before sprouting?

Which seeds germinate the fastest? The slowest?

How long does it take for the plants to grow to 6 inches high?

Related activities: BIS 2, BIS 21, BIS 24, BIS 43, BIS 78, SS 7

Spooling Along—Studying Motion   BIS **79**

Materials: 35-mm film canister; rubber bands (shorter than the length of the film canister); toothpicks; pipe cleaner; spherical plastic bead; pencil or drinking straw **More:** rubber bands of different sizes; board; books

Procedure:

* Punch a hole in each end of a film canister. Thread a rubber band through the canister. (Use a pipe cleaner to draw the rubber band through.)

* Use a toothpick to keep the rubber band from sliding back through the canister. (See illustration.)

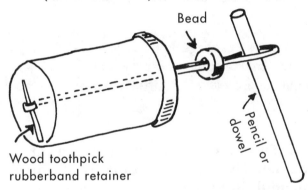

Bead

Pencil or dowel

Wood toothpick
rubberband retainer

* Thread a bead onto the rubber band. Between the bead and the end of the rubber band, insert a pencil to stabilize the spool mobile. (Position the pencil so that $\frac{3}{4}$ of it is below the rubber band.)

* Remove the pipe cleaner.

* Crank the rubber band and observe the spool mobile's actions.

  Does the spool move in a straight line?

  How can you make a spool mobile travel in a straight line? In a curved path?

  Can you construct a multiple-spooled device? How does this affect the distance traveled?

  How can you reduce the friction of the spool mobile? Does this affect the distance traveled?

  How could you improve the traction of the mobile?

More:

- Vary the number of rubber band cranks, the thickness of rubber bands, and the number of rubber bands. Observe the motion of the spool mobile in all cases.

  Does doubling the number of cranks result in twice the distance traveled?

  Does doubling the thickness of the rubber band change the distance traveled?

  Does using two rubber bands affect the distance traveled? Three rubber bands?

- Use the books to make the board an inclined plane for the mobile to travel on and vary the angle of the plane.

  What happens to the mobile as the angle of the plane is increased?

Related activities: BIS 37, BIS 60, BIS 65, BIS 77, BIS 80

BIS **80**

Acid? Base? You Decide! Testing for Acids and Bases

Materials: head of red cabbage; knife; large cooking pot; stove or hot plate; strainer; baking soda; vinegar; water; 3 small jars **More:** coffee filter; liquid soap; juices (orange, carrot, and tomato); soft drink; milk

WARNING: This activity involves heat. Be careful not to burn yourself. This activity should be performed only when an adult is present.

Procedure:

- Shred about $\frac{1}{2}$ to $\frac{3}{4}$ of the head of cabbage.

- Put the cabbage into a pot and add enough water to cover it. Bring this to a boil, then reduce the heat and let the cabbage simmer until the leaves turn whitish and the water is a deep purple. (This should take about 10 minutes.)

- Strain the juice and refrigerate it. (If not refrigerated, it will spoil.)

- Put a teaspoon of baking soda into a small jar. Pour some vinegar into a second jar. Pour some water into a third jar.

- Add $\frac{1}{2}$ to 1 teaspoon of cabbage juice to each jar.

  What color changes did you observe?

The water (neutral) turns purplish. The baking soda (a base) turns green, and the vinegar (an acid) turns red.

- Make indicator paper by soaking strips of coffee filter in the red cabbage juice for about 20–30 minutes. Remove the paper and let it dry overnight.

- Dip a strip of filter paper in each liquid—soap; lemon, orange, carrot, and tomato juice; soft drink; milk.

    Which were acids? Which were bases?

Related activities: BIS 9, BIS 15, BIS 32, BIS 35, BIS 62

Free as a Frier Fly–Learning about Genetics

BIS **81**

Materials: copies of the imaginary frier fly A and B (pages 109 and 110); sheet of paper

Procedure:

- Look at frier flies A and B. Observe and describe one of the flies. Then compare the two.

    How are they alike? How are they different?

- Print a large *D* (dominant) on each of the 7 sections of frier fly A.

- Label all seven sections of frier fly B's features with a small *d* (recessive).

- Now cut up the 2 frier fly diagrams and mix up the pieces. Assemble a new frier fly using any mixture of *D* (dominant) features and *d* (recessive) features.

- Paste the new frier fly on another sheet of paper and label it frier fly O.

- Work with a partner to make a new frier fly. Each of you will contribute your frier fly O as a parent.

- Record this information on a chart.

Facts to know:

◇ Offspring usually resemble their parents in certain major respects but differ from their parents in many minor respects.

◇ Offspring do not inherit features such as curly hair or blue eyes, but they do inherit genes that give rise to curly hair or blue eyes.

◇ Each parent passes on one set of genes to the offspring. Each feature is influenced by at least one gene from each parent.

◇ Genes that control the production of a feature are called <u>dominant</u> (denoted by <u>D</u>). Those genes whose features can be hidden by another are called <u>recessive</u> (denoted by <u>d</u>).

◇◇◇

Feature	Contribution from Parent 1	Contribution from Parent 2	Offspring's Features
1. body	fluted ( )	not fluted ( )	_____ ( )
2. wings	striped ( )	not striped ( )	_____ ( )
3. tail	sharp ( )	blunted ( )	_____ ( )
4. legs	cylindrical ( )	curly ( )	_____ ( )
5. neck	threaded ( )	bayonet ( )	_____ ( )
6. antenna	split ( )	whole ( )	_____ ( )
7. nose	2-pronged ( )	3-pronged ( )	_____ ( )

- Record the letter designation (D or d) for each feature from each frier fly O parent. One (D) in any feature will make that feature dominant (D) for the offspring. Two (d) in any feature will make that feature recessive (d) for the offspring.

What would the frier fly offspring generated from the parent O frier flies look like?

Can you write a description of the offspring, detailing the features?

What would the next generation look like from other frier fly parent matches?

Related activities: BIS 1, BIS 66

108

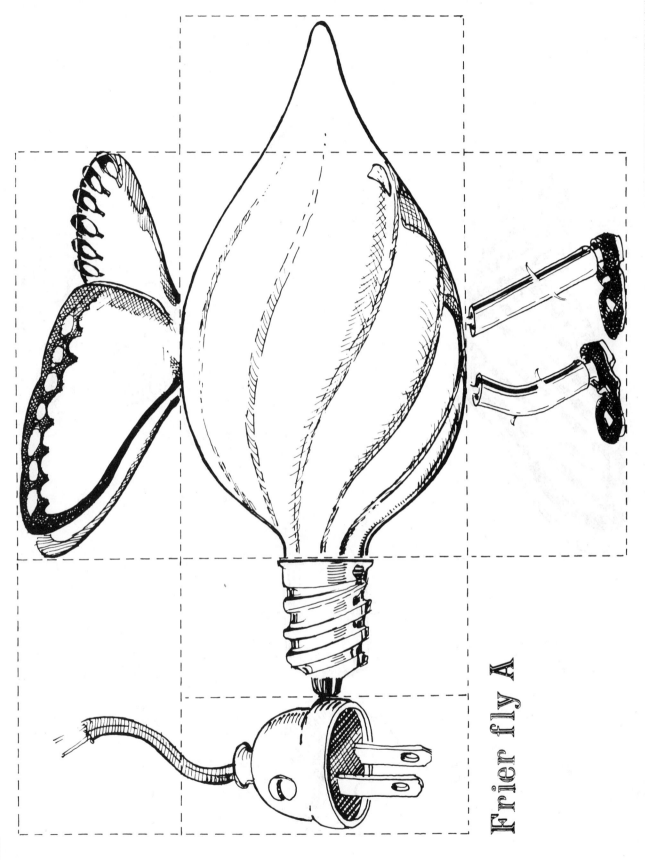

Frier fly A

109

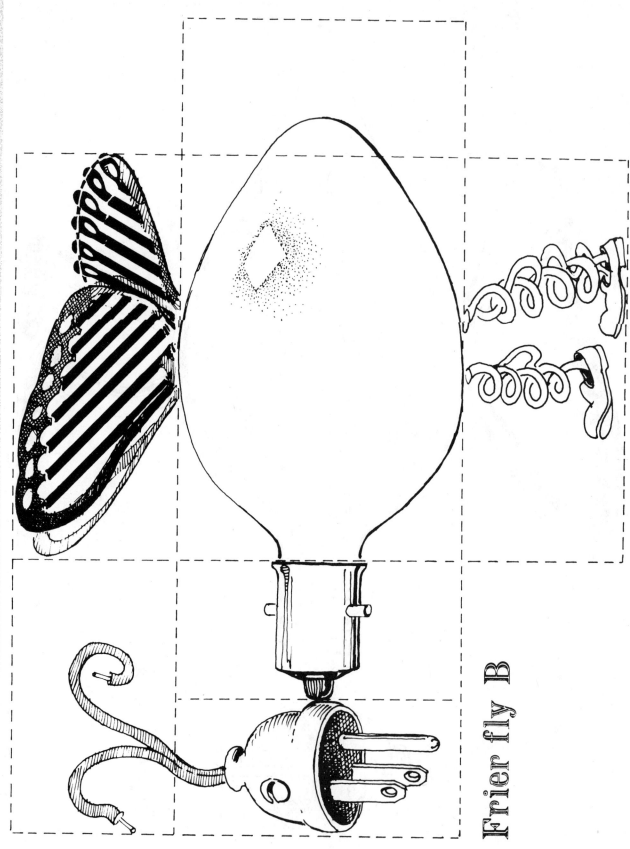

Frier fly B

A Vitamin C Tester

Materials: cornstarch; small cooking pot; stove or hot plate; glass jar; iodine; dropper; 8 small cups; teaspoon; various fruits and vegetables (orange, green pepper, lemon, grapefruit, potato); nuts; rice; water **More:** data table (below)

WARNING: This activity involves heat. Be careful not to burn yourself. This activity should be performed only when an adult is present.

Iodine is poisonous. Do **NOT** taste any food with iodine on it.

Procedure:

- Add 1 teaspoon of cornstarch to the pot with a small amount of warm water. Stir and bring to a boil.

- When the liquid is cooled, pour it into the glass jar. Add 1 or 2 drops of iodine. (The mixture will turn dark blue or black. This is your Vitamin C indicator.)

- Pour small amounts of the indicator into each of the several cups. Drop a small amount of one type of food into each cup.

- Describe your observations for each container.

  Which foods contain Vitamin C? Which do not?

More:

- Prepare a chart that illustrates the number of drops of Vitamin C indicator needed to cause a color change.

  Which food needs the least drops? The most?

  What can you infer from this information?

Number of drops	Mass and name of food used, grams

Related activities: BIS 39, BIS 45, BIS 53, BIS 80

Density and Specific Gravity

> **Materials:** spoon; clear drinking glass; tea bag; small cooking pot; hot plate; ground pepper; water **More:** corn syrup; water; meat baster; cooking oil; drinking glasses; ice cubes; molasses; rubbing alcohol; nail; cork; candle; aluminum foil; bowl; small clear bottle

Facts to know:

◇ <u>Density</u> is mass per unit of volume. Usually the unit volume selected is 1 cubic centimeter because the mass of this volume of water is 1 gram.

◇ <u>Specific gravity</u> is a number derived from the ratio between the weight of a substance and the weight of an equal volume of water at 4° C.

◇ Pure water is assigned a specific gravity of 1. The specific gravity of other substances is compared to water. If a substance has a specific gravity of 2, it is twice as heavy as water.

◇◇◇

When objects are heated, they expand and become lighter. Hot or warm water is lighter than cold water.

Procedure:

● Place the spoon into the empty glass.

> **WARNING: Wear safety goggles for the next step.**

● Carefully fill the glass with hot, almost boiling, water. (The spoon absorbs and conducts heat so that the glass will not crack.)

● Carefully hang a tea bag over the edge of the glass so that it is submerged in the water.

> *What do you observe? What sinks to the bottom of the glass?*
>
> *Which is heavier, the clear water or the dissolved tea?*

● Boil a pot of water.

● When the water is boiling, add some pepper.

> *What pattern of water movement do you observe? Can you explain why?*

More:

● Pour a 1-inch layer of corn syrup into the drinking glass.

● Slowly add a 1-inch layer of water. (Use a meat baster to dribble the water onto the wall of the glass.)

● Then slowly add a 1-inch layer of cooking oil.

> *What do you observe?*

● Place a 1-inch layer of cooking oil in another glass. Place 1 ice cube in the cooking oil.

● Observe the ice cube as it melts.

> *What does the ice do when you place it in the glass?*
>
> *What happens as the ice melts?*
>
> *What does this tell you about the densities of oil, ice, and water?*
>
> *How can you explain what you see?*

- Gently pour equal amounts of cooking oil, molasses, and water into a glass.

  Which liquid is the lightest? The heaviest?

- Place a nail, a cork, and a piece of wax candle in the glass.

  Which objects sink? Which float? Which float but are immersed?

- Carefully add rubbing alcohol.

  What does this do to the equilibrium of the system?

- Cut 2 equal-size squares (approximately 10 cm square) from the aluminum foil. Shape one piece into a compact ball. Shape the other square into a flat boat.

  Do these two object have the same mass?

- Place your aluminum boat and sphere in a bowl of water.

  What do you observe?

  Do both objects have the same densities? What else do you think is involved?

- Pour water into a glass. Add a drop or two of cooking oil.

- Slowly add alcohol by pouring it down the sides of the glass.

  Which liquid is on top? In the middle? On the bottom?

  What do you observe about the oil?

  What does this tell you about the density of oil? Of alcohol?

- Fill the small bottle about $\frac{1}{2}$ full with rubbing alcohol.

- Add a few drops of cooking oil.

- Carefully add water, a little at a time, capping the bottle each time, and gently shake to mix the water and alcohol.

- Observe the behavior of the oil droplets each time.

  What do you observe?

  What happens to the density of the alcohol/water solution?

  Does this explain your observations?

  Would the addition of soapy water influence the results?

Related activities: BIS 20, BIS 33, BIS 74

Substances with specific gravities <u>less than</u> 1 float in water.

Substances with specific gravities <u>more than</u> 1 sink in water.

Substances with specific gravities <u>equal to</u> 1 float at the surface but remain immersed in water.

Ice is less dense than water, and oil. When ice melts, its density changes. It now has a density greater than ice or oil and sinks to the bottom.

Oil is less dense than water, and alcohol is less dense than either oil or water.

The "Are You Alive" Carbon Dioxide Test

Facts to know:

◇ The air you breathe contains oxygen and a small amount of carbon dioxide.

◇ You breathe out carbon dioxide when you exhale.

◇◇◇

The liquid turned milky because calcium carbonate formed when the carbon dioxide in your breath combined with the limewater. If you blow for too long, the milky limewater will turn clear. Excess carbon dioxide changes the calcium carbonate to calcium bicarbonate.

Materials: limewater (available in drugstores OR made by adding a teaspoon of slaked lime to a quart of water, shaking vigorously, and allowing to settle for 2 to 3 hours); small clear container; soda straw **More:** pint jar; vinegar; baking soda; candle; aluminum pan; cardboard; 2 identical-size paper bags; meter stick; string

WARNING: Do not inhale or swallow the limewater.

Procedure:

⟐ Pour a small amount of limewater into a container.

⟐ Exhale your breath into the liquid through a straw.

⟐ Record the time it takes to make the limewater turn milky.

What do you observe about the liquid?

What happens as you continue to exhale into the liquid?

⟐ Exercise vigorously for 15 to 20 minutes. Then repeat the activity.

⟐ Compare the time it took to turn the limewater milky before exercise to the time it took after exercise.

What can you conclude about exercising and the rate of carbon dioxide exhalation?

More:

⟐ Pour $\frac{1}{4}$ cup of vinegar into the pint jar. Add 1 teaspoon of baking soda.

⟐ Place a flat piece of cardboard over the mouth of the jar to keep gas from escaping.

⟐ Stand a lighted candle in the aluminum pan. Make a cardboard trough.

WARNING: Burning candles are dangerous. This activity should be performed only when an adult is present.

⟐ Uncover the jar and quickly pour the gas (not the solids or liquids) into the trough positioned above and directed toward the flame.

What do you observe about the flame?

Can you infer what gas was made from vinegar and baking soda?

⟐ Use a piece of string to suspend the meter stick from the ceiling. Adjust the position of the string so that the meter stick is horizontal. (It is now balanced.)

- Attach a piece of string to each paper bag.

- Suspend the two bags, one at each end of the meter stick.

- Bring the two bags in balance, so that the meter stick is again horizontal. (Both bags are now filled with air.)

- Prepare several pints of carbon dioxide and pour the gas only into one of the bags.

    What do you observe? Is carbon dioxide heavier than air?

Related activities: BIS 21, BIS 47, CSR 13

Star Clock and Calendar– Investigating the Movement of Constellations

BIS **85**

Materials: umbrella; white chalk; chart of constellations (Big Dipper, Little Dipper, Cassiopeia) **More:** chalk; umbrella; microscope slide; microscope; petroleum jelly; metric balance

Facts to know:

◇ The earth, moving in its orbit about the sun, causes the various constellations to seem to move across the sky.

◇ The stars appear to rotate one full turn in 24 hours and to make one full revolution in one year.

◇◇◇

Procedure:

- Place an umbrella directly over your head. Think of the North Star as being positioned exactly at the top of the umbrella shaft where it exits the umbrella.

- Divide the underside of the umbrella into four quadrants, and chalk in the Big Dipper, the Little Dipper, and Cassiopeia.

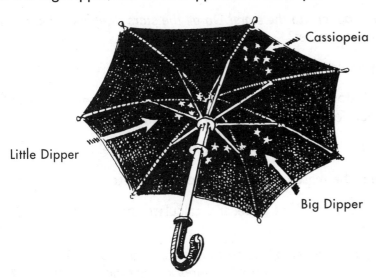

Cassiopeia

Little Dipper

Big Dipper

- Place the umbrella over your head.

- Hold the umbrella motionless and rotate (walk) under the umbrella in a counterclockwise direction, imitating the motion of the earth.

    In what direction do the stars appear to move?

- Standing under the umbrella, orient the constellation Cassiopeia in a northerly direction.

- Simulate the rotation of the earth under the umbrella. (Remember it takes the earth 24 hours for one rotation.) In 6 hours, you would move through an area equal to $\frac{1}{4}$ of the umbrella area (or 90° or 1 quadrant).

    Where does Cassiopeia appear to be in 6 hours?

    How many degrees do you travel in 1 hour?

    Where would Cassiopeia be after one full rotation?

    Suppose you fell asleep under the stars while camping and you noted Cassiopeia's position at 10:00 P.M. When you woke up Cassiopeia appeared to have moved 90°; what time would it be?

- Note the position of the Big Dipper. Record the time, date, and relative position of this constellation.

- Repeat this procedure at the same time and day each month for several months.

    What do you observe about the position of the constellations?

    What can you infer about the path of the Big Dipper?

    Can you predict the location of this constellation 6 months from your initial observation? 9 months? 1 year?

More:

- Chalk in some additional stars near the outer edges of the umbrella. Tilt the umbrella 23° to coincide with the earth's axis and look straight ahead. Rotate the umbrella.

    What happens to the stars? Do all the stars disappear? Do all the stars rise and set?

- Apply a thin coat of petroleum jelly to the microscope slide.

- Place it outdoors exposed to the sky in a location where it will be undisturbed for 24 hours to catch micrometeorites.

- Examine the slide under a compound microscope.

- Determine the mass of the collected micrometeorites.

- Measure the area of the slide, and calculate the mass per square centimeter.

    If the total surface of the earth is calculated at 5.1×10^{18} cm², what is the mass of micrometeorites striking the earth every 24 hours?

Related activities: BIS 15, BIS 56, SS 15

How Much Dust is in the Air? BIS 86

Materials: 3 1-gallon, wide-mouth glass jars; 3 pans; 2 gallons of distilled water; three 3-quart pans; wire; window screening; metric balance; heat source such as alcohol lamp or stove **More:** vacuum cleaner; filter paper; hand lens or microscope; nylon stocking; cardboard; rubber bands; pieces of wood; hammer; nails

WARNING: This activity involves the use of heat. Be careful not to burn yourself. This activity should be done only when an adult is present.

Procedure:

* Pour a quart of distilled water into each of the 3 jars and mark the water level.

* Label the jars and pans 1, 2, and 3. Weigh and record the mass of each of the empty pans.

* Cover the top of each jar with a piece of screening folded down over the mouth. Fasten the screen with wire.

* Set the jars outside, about 5 feet above the ground, in an area you wish to test. (Since you will need to expose the jars for 30 days, make sure they are in a place that will not be disturbed by people or animals.)

* Check each jar daily, record your observations, and add distilled water to keep the water at the level marked.

* After 30 days, pour the water from jar 1 into pan 1. Weigh the pan containing the water and dust and record the mass.

* Place the pan on a heat source, and carefully evaporate the water. Weigh the pan after the water is evaporated. Record the mass.

* Repeat for jars 2 and 3. (You may need to rinse out each jar with additional distilled water to get all the material out.)

* Prepare a data table and record: (1) the mass of the pan with the water and dust; (2) the mass of the pan and the dust; and (3) the mass of the pan.

* Subtract to obtain the mass of the dust in milligrams. (This is the amount of milligrams collected in 30 days—one month—per the surface area of your jars.)

   How does your data compare with your classmates' data?

   Who collected the most dust? The least?

More:

- Place a piece of filter paper over the hose opening of a vacuum cleaner. Turn on the vacuum and collect dust in your classroom. Examine the filter paper through a hand lens or microscope. Try to identify some of the particles.

- Use the vacuum cleaner to test other locations and compare these areas to your classroom.

    Which has the least dust? The most dust?

- Mount squares of nylon stocking on cardboard frames. Hang them up outside your house or school in areas where you want to test for air pollution's effect on clothing.

- Examine the nylon with a hand lens after a few days. (Damage appears as broken fibers.)

    How do your results compare to your classmates' results?

    Which location shows the most damage to the nylon? The least?

- Hammer 2 nails into a piece of wood.

- Stretch a rubber band between the nails. (Ozone will cause the rubber band to crack and break.)

- Make 2 more of the same rubber band apparatus.

- Place the first near an electric appliance; the second indoors; the third outdoors.

- Record how long it takes for your rubber bands to break. Compare your results to your classmates' results.

    Which rubber band broke the fastest? The slowest?

    What does this tell you about the amount of ozone in the air in different locations?

Related activities: BIS 63, SS 12

Osmosis: Crossing the Impermeable Barrier

Materials: 4 raw eggs in shells; 4 jars with 7- to 8-cm openings and caps; 4 pints white vinegar; 4 pints white corn syrup **More:** 2 raw eggs in shells; corn syrup; salt water; jars; dried fruit; 2 plastic containers

Procedure:

- Set up four jars: Jar 1—all vinegar; Jar 2—2 parts vinegar and 1 part water; Jar 3— 2 parts vinegar and 2 parts water; Jar 4—all water. Carefully place one raw egg (still in the shell) in each jar, making sure that each egg is completely covered by the liquid.

- Cap the jars and observe the eggs after 1 hour, 3 hours, 1 day, and 2 days. Record your observations.

     Do you observe bubbling in the jar with vinegar (Jar 1)?

     Do the eggs float in the vinegar solutions (Jars 2 and 3)?

     Do you also observe that in each of the vinegar-water combinations, the hard eggshell dissolves and the egg grows larger? What can you infer?

- After 2 days, pour off the vinegar in Jar 1, put clear corn syrup in the jar, and observe the egg for a day. Record observations after 1 hour, 3 hours, and 1 day.

     Do you observe that the egg in the syrup became indented?

     Why does this happen?

     How does the eggshell compare to a cell wall?

More:

- Place 1 egg in a syrup solution in a jar and another egg in a salt solution.

     What do you observe?

     Why doesn't the syrup go through the shell of the egg?

     Can you make a diagram to explain your answer?

- Put salt water in 1 plastic container and plain water in another.

- Place dried fruit (apricots, prunes, or apples) in each container.

- Observe each container after 1 hour, 3 hours, 12 hours, and 1 day.

     Can you explain why the fruit in the salt water does not change?

A cell wall allows certain materials to pass through the wall to the cell's interior. This is called a <u>semipermeable membrane.</u>

Related activities: BIS 47

Retinal Retentions

> **Materials:** thin, stiff cardboard; ruler; red, blue, yellow markers; rubber bands **More:** cardboard; rubber bands; any color marker

Procedure:

- Cut a 2-inch diameter disk from the cardboard.

- Color one side of the disk red and the other side blue.

- Punch 2 holes opposite each other in the outer area of the disk. Thread rubber bands through the holes.

- Wind the apparatus up by twisting the rubber bands and release.

    What color or colors do you observe? Can you explain why?

- Cut another 2-inch diameter disk from cardboard.

- Divide one side of the disk into four equal quadrants. Color one quadrant blue, and the adjacent quadrant yellow, then the next quadrant blue, and the last quadrant yellow.

- Punch 2 holes near the center of the disk and thread rubber bands through the holes.

- Wind up the apparatus by twisting the rubber bands and then releasing them.

    What color or colors do you observe? Can you explain why?

More:

- Cut a 2-inch square from the cardboard. Draw a picture of a fish on one side and a picture of a fishbowl on the other side.

- Punch 2 holes near the edge, at opposite ends of the cardboard. Thread rubber bands through the holes.

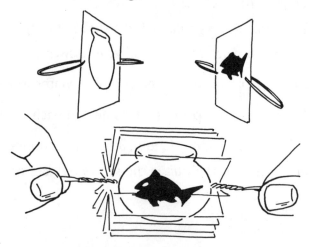

The retina in your eye can hold a viewed image for a split second after the image is gone from sight. This is called <u>retinal retention.</u>

- Wind up the device by twisting the rubber bands and release.

   What do you observe? Why?

Related activities: BIS 36, BIS 64

Fall Leaf Colors—Chromatography

> **Materials:** green leaves; rubbing alcohol; white paper towel or filter paper; soda straw; plastic container; plastic wrap; glass jar; spoon
> **More:** fall leaves from maple, sycamore, or ash; rubbing alcohol; white paper towel; soda straw; glass jar; plastic container; spoon

WARNING: Keep alcohol away from an open flame. Do not drink the alcohol. Only use alcohol in a well-ventilated area.

Procedure:

- Place some crushed, green leaves into the plastic container. Cover the leaves with rubbing alcohol.

- Gently mash the leaves with a spoon. Then, cover the container with plastic wrap.

- Leave this mixture undisturbed for 15 to 20 minutes. Drain off and keep the liquid and throw away the crushed leaves.

- Place some of the leaf liquid into the glass jar.

- Cut a strip of filter paper or paper toweling about 2 cm wide and long enough to reach the bottom of the jar.

- Wrap the strip over the straw so that it hangs into the jar. (The paper strip should be barely submerged in the liquid.)

- Cover the jar with plastic wrap for 15 minutes.

   What do you observe? Where do the colors come from?

More:

- Repeat the activity with fall leaves.

   What do you observe? Are your results the same? Why or why not?

Related activities: BIS 12, BIS 47, BIS 51, BIS 53

The coloring comes from plant cells in the leaves. The visible colors are green, yellow, and reddish brown. In the fall the green pigments disappear, and yellow and red pigments are most common.

Science with a Sheet of Paper

Materials: $8\frac{1}{2}$ x 11-inch sheets of paper; newspaper; brown paper bag; bond paper; jar; yardstick or meter stick **More:** sheets of paper; hole punch; books for weights

Procedure:

* Devise a way to find the mass of an $8\frac{1}{2}$ x 11-inch sheet of paper.

    Can you weigh 1 sheet? Is it easier to find the mass if you weigh more than 1 sheet and divide to find the mass of 1 sheet?

    What is the mass of 1 sheet?

* Determine the area of an $8\frac{1}{2}$ x 11-inch sheet of paper. Draw different geometric shapes on the paper and cut them out.

    What is the area of the remaining paper?

* Use two $8\frac{1}{2}$ x 11-inch sheets of paper to construct 2 cylinders. Make one cylinder 11 inches high with a base circle whose circumference is $8\frac{1}{2}$ inches.

* Make the other cylinder $8\frac{1}{2}$ inches high with a base circle whose circumference is 11 inches.

    Do you think that these 2 cylinders have the same volume or different volumes?

* Make an inference, then calculate the volume of each cylinder.

    Are your predictions correct? Are the volumes of the 2 cylinders equal?

* Draw geometric tangram shapes to completely fill an $8\frac{1}{2}$ x 11-inch sheet of paper.

* Compare your results with your classmates' results.

    What is the fewest number of shapes?

    How many shapes have an area of 4 square inches? 2 square inches?

* Fold an $8\frac{1}{2}$ x 11-inch sheet of paper as many times as you can.

    How many times can you fold it?

    Do you think the number of folds is the same for all sizes of paper?

* Devise a way to compare how much water different kinds of paper can absorb. Try bond paper, paper toweling, newspaper, and brown bag paper.

    Which paper absorbs the most water? The least?

The number of times a sheet of paper can be folded depends on the thickness of the paper. Most can be folded no more than nine times.

Whatever the original size of the paper, the paper is being folded at the same rate. The area of the paper is divided in half with each fold.

- Drop a sheet of paper from a measured height.

  How long does it take to reach ground level?

- Roll the same sheet into a ball, and drop it from the same height.

  How long does it take to reach ground level?

  How does this compare to the sheet of paper? Which is more resistant to the flow of air?

- Place a large sheet of newspaper over the yardstick or meter stick. Place the paper at the edge of the table with the stick extending $\frac{1}{2}$ of its length beyond the table.

- With the edge of your hand, hit the stick at about the midpoint of the extended part of the stick.

  What happens as the result of your blow?

  Why doesn't the newspaper sheet lift into the air? What is exerting a force on the newspaper sheet?

- Calculate the number of square inches contained in the surface area of your newspaper sheet. (The air pressure on the paper is approximately 14.7 pounds per square inch.)

  How many total pounds of air pressure are bearing down on the entire surface area of the newspaper sheet?

More:

- Construct 4 structures out of paper (as shown in the illustration).

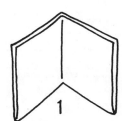 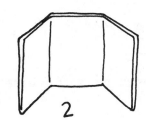  

- Weight each structure with books.

  How much weight will each structure bear?

  Which structure holds the most weight? The least?

  How does the number of creases or folds relate to the ability of each structure to support more weight?

  Does overlapping a crease alter how much weight a structure can support?

  Does taping or glueing the overlap change the amount of weight?

  Does changing the geometric shape change how much the structure can support? Which change seems to support the greatest amount of weight?

  Does adding internal crossmembers change the structural strength?

How much weight will a creatively folded $8\frac{1}{2}$ x 11-inch sheet of paper support?

How might each structure be changed so that it could support a greater weight?

- Cut 5 rectangles out of paper, approximately $5\frac{1}{2}$ x $8\frac{1}{2}$ inches each. Fold 1 rectangle in half. Use the hole punch to punch a hole in the center of the folded rectangle.

- Predict where the holes will appear when the folded sheet is opened to its original size.

- Fold another rectangle twice. Punch a hole in the middle.

- Predict where the holes will appear on the paper when this double-folded sheet is opened to its original size.

- Repeat this for each remaining rectangle, increasing the number of folds one more each time. Predict the results in each case.

    Are your predictions correct?

    Can you predict the results for a sixth rectangle without actually punching a hole in it?

    Devise a formula relating the number of folds to the number of holes punched.

Related activities: BIS 20, BIS 23, BIS 61, BIS 71, BIS 77, BIS 83

BIS 91

Rock or Mineral? A Puzzle

Materials: tagboard; patterns of geometric shapes (page 125)
More: completed puzzles

Facts to know:

◇ A <u>mineral</u> is a naturally occurring substance that has a characteristic internal structure formed by regularly arranged atoms or ions within it. A mineral's chemical composition and physical properties either are fixed or vary within a definite range.

◇ A rock is an aggregate of minerals.

◇◇◇

Procedure:

- Make 16 cutouts of each of the 4 geometric shapes (trace the shapes in the illustration).

- Color 4 cutouts of each shape white and label them Quartz. Color 4 of each shape pink and label them Feldspar. Color 4 of each shape black and label them Mica. Color the last 4 of each shape green and label them Hornblende.

- Put your cutouts together like a puzzle. Compare your completed puzzle with a classmate's puzzle.

    Is your puzzle a rock or a mineral? How can you tell?

    Is your puzzle made with one color of cutouts? More than one color?

    How does a rock differ from a mineral? Which is which?

More:

* Estimate the percentages of each of your puzzle's mineral components.

* Compare your results to your classmates' results.

    Who has the largest percentage of feldspar? Of quartz?

Adapted from Alfred DeVito, *Rocks and Minerals—A Puzzle, Science Activities*, Vol. 3(3), April 1970, pp. 35–37. By permission.

Related activities: BIS 21, BIS 51

The average granite contains 60% feldspar, 30% quartz, and 10% dark minerals (biotite, mica, or hornblende).

If the finished puzzle is entirely composed of one color of cutouts, it represents a cross section of a mineral. If two or more different colored cutouts are used, the cross section will represent a rock.

SHOESTRING SCIENCING

More for Less

How many times have you made a major expenditure for science equipment that annihilated your science allotment? How many times have you received the equipment with wild anticipation, only to find that you could have duplicated the materials or gotten comparable ones for a tenth or a twentieth of the original cost? Convenience costs money. Catalog purchasing is tidy, convenient, and costly. Sometimes it is a disaster. Occasionally, however, it is an absolute necessity.

By and large, you can realize tremendous savings by purchasing your own science materials or by purchasing the components to construct equipment of your own design. This flexibility allows you to acquire exactly what you need in the quantities you need for your class. One innovative teacher in a large suburban school saved her district more than $200,000 in one year by making equipment for district-wide use and having children help her assemble the materials.

Catalog shopping can be replaced by repeated tours of supermarkets, lumberyards, junkyards, garage sales, discount stores, drugstores, auctions, stationery stores, cellars, attics, school-supply cabinets, and home closets. This takes time and energy, but the results are well worth the effort. Many school-supply closets contain a lot of science equipment that has yet to be discovered by teachers, including microscopes, beakers, test tubes, and tuning forks, all yours for the investigating.

Section Two of *Creative Sciencing,* called Shoestring Sciencing (SS), is designed to provide you with many ideas that involve a minimum of equipment and cost for a maximum of science. Shoestring sciencers collect and save almost everything, from string to aluminum foil. You never know when you may need 60 baby food jars or 45 aluminum pie pans immediately. Anticipate and be ready. To succeed in creative sciencing inexpensively, adopt the substitution habit—a baby food jar can stand in for scientific glassware.

WHEN YOU NEED	SUBSTITUTE
Aquaria	Gallon jars
Crayfish homes	Plastic swimming pools
Flashlight casings	Toilet paper rolls
Vials	Used pill bottles
Droppers	Soda straws
Weights	Fishing sinkers
Spheres	Marbles
Containers	Coffee, film, tobacco, tuna, and soup cans
Wheels	Skates, bicycles, toy cars
Mirrors	Aluminum foil on cardboard
Graduated cylinders	Baby bottles or medicine cups
Shelves	Cardboard boxes
Density objects	Clay, copper tubing or pipe, iron or aluminum nails
Mobile supports	Coat hangers
Dowels	Broomsticks
Trays	TV-dinner trays, pie pans, margarine tubs, school lunch trays
Jars	Pop bottles, wine bottles, mayonnaise jars, pickle jars, ketchup bottles
Measuring sticks	Scrap lumber, licorice, string, or straws
Wire or string	Fishing line
Screening	Nylon stockings
Stirring rods	Popsicle sticks
Scoops or shovels	Plastic bleach bottles
Culture dishes	Plastic margarine tubs
Timers	Old alarm clock

Ask the students to bring in needed articles. Advertise in the school newspaper (you may have to start your own). Parents can provide many things you need, from corks to old typewriters. One teacher inherited an old but usable sewing machine. At the end of the year you can have one huge garage sale.

Activities in this section will get you started in creative sciencing, on a shoestring if necessary. We hope that you can extend the intent and purpose of shoestring sciencing to shoestring art, mathematics, social studies, and anywhere else it will do some good.

Recycling Helps Science Education

Examining what you throw out as you clear the house of daily trash can furnish a steady supply of science equipment—all free and expendable.

To help you assemble some of the hardware that teaching science requires, we suggest that you start collecting materials now. Save everything that looks remotely usable, even though its use may not be immediately apparent.

Who knows how many materials could be recycled from trash into your science program? This list is a beginning.

Glassware

Pop bottles

Catsup bottles

Wine bottles plus corks

Mayonnaise jars

Pickle jars

Containers

Cups (plastic and paper)

Egg cartons

Gallon jugs (glass and plastic)

Coffee cans

Margarine tubs

Small plastic berry containers

Aluminum TV dinner trays

Pie pans

Plastic containers

Wooden objects

Spools

Broomsticks

Dowels

Curtain rods

Clothespins

Scraps of wood

Miscellaneous

Old golf and tennis balls

Marbles

Balloons

Bottle tops or caps

Boxes (plastic, cigar, cardboard)

Aluminum foil

Cellophane wrap

Insulation materials

Parts from old toys and kits

Leftover paints

Charcoal

Milk cartons

Paraffin

Clay

Soda straws

Blotters

BB shot

Crayons

Old pots, pans, trays

Flowerpots

Flooring squares

Ceramic tiles

Copper pipe and tubing

Nuts and bolts

Screws and nails

Washers

Leather belts, purses,
and wallets

Coat hangers

Old 35-mm slides

Film canisters

Coffee cans

Cardboard

String

Fishing weights

Straight pins, tacks,
thumbtacks

Old radios and TVs

Screening

Elastic materials

Pieces of fabric such
as corduroy, silk, cotton

Sand, dirt, gravel, and
sawdust

Mirrors

Eyeglass lenses

Springs

Wire

Droppers

Baby bottles

Wheels (skate, bicycle)

Old manila folders

Scissors

Old clocks

Stirring rods

Old nylon stockings

Pill bottles

Batteries

Paper tubes (toilet, towel)

Cheesecloth

Thread

Iron filings

Flashlights

Adapted from Alfred DeVito, "Found Science Equipment." *Science Activities,
Vol.8(5),* January 1973, p. 15. By permission.

Related activity: BIS 44

Using Playground Equipment to Explain Abstract Ideas

Science is more often taught indoors than outdoors for many reasons, yet the inside is not necessarily the best place to practice sciencing. The outdoors can be a cornucopia for making abstract ideas concrete. When you're teaching difficult science concepts, playground equipment can be used to advantage.

The Seesaw

- The seesaw can be used as a mammoth equal-arm balance, with students of equal (or unequal) weights appropriately positioned to bring the balance into equilibrium. You could position yourself on one end and see if one or more students at the opposite end can balance the teeter-totter.

- It can be an example of the lever or inclined plane.

- It can teach about efficiency of machines.

The Swing

- The playground swing is a pendulum. Students swinging can be a dramatic lesson about pendulums. They become part of the pendulum's mass.

- Students can experience motion, rest, vibration, frequency, displacement, and amplitude.

- Students can also experience positions in a complete vibration, reinforcing understanding of potential energy and kinetic energy.

The Slide

- A slide will help you demonstrate an inclined plane when you roll objects of varying masses down the inclined plane. Everyone can observe the time and distance and calculate the rate of speed.

- You can change the slide's surface to reduce or increase friction and measure the effect on speed.

The Jungle Bars

- The equally spaced, intersecting bars nicely introduce two-dimensional and three-dimensional space.

- You can use the bars as a three-dimensional grid system. Students can then locate a point in space or designate coordinates (*x*, *y*, and *z*) of a point in space.

The Merry-Go-Round

* This apparatus can help you get across the ideas of rotation and revolution. (A bicycle wheel is a suitable substitute.)

* Uniform circular motion, rotary motion, angular velocity, angular acceleration, moment of inertia, angular momentum, Newton's three laws of motion, and other notions can be extracted from the spinning wheel or the merry-go-round.

* In how many ways can you work playground equipment at your local school into creative sciencing ventures?

Related activities: BIS 4, SS 12

Plaster of Paris Constructs

Plaster of Paris can be bought in hardware stores, hobby shops, art supply houses, or discount stores and is excellent for preparing casts or molds. It comes as a fine white powder that you add to water (NOT THE REVERSE) until it has a pasty consistency. Because it usually hardens (sets up) in about 10 to 15 minutes, you should have your project well in mind before mixing the plaster with water. It generates heat while it is drying, so caution is recommended.

> **WARNING:** Wash your hands immediately after using plaster of Paris and keep it away from all mucous membranes, eyes included!
>
> Any remaining material should **NOT** be washed down a sink drain; put it in a trash container designed for solid waste.

Some Ideas

* Make casts of animal tracks; tire tracks; people tracks; people casts, including hands, fingers, elbows, knees, toes, and feet; and plant tracks.

* Make models of mountains, hills, and valleys.

* Make objects for observation of various shapes, sizes, colors, and weights.

* Make casts from plaster of Paris to which you've added food coloring, sand, soil, gravel, or rocks.

* Make varying thicknesses of the plaster of Paris. Let your students see if they can make buildings or homes.

- Make plaster of Paris maps of cities, states, and nations. Try maps of highways, rivers, rock formations, and topographic maps.

- Make impressions in plaster of Paris casts before they harden. Use chicken wire (press down and remove it); assorted sizes of wire screening; and nuts, bolts, screws, nails, and washers to make impressions. Have students make inferences about the object used to make the impression.

Related activities: BIS 30, SS 6, SS 10, SS 17

SS 4

Building a "Right Answer" Light Indicator

Materials: 2-pound plastic butter container (or a similar-size container); 2 D-cell batteries; bell wire; 2 probes (from electrical supply house or hardware store); flashlight bulb; soldering iron; solder; aluminum foil; file folders (old greeting cards or index cards can be used instead); masking tape; hole punch

The Indicator

- Attach a wire from the positive side of one battery to the negative side of the other battery. Then place the batteries in the butter container. (See diagram.)

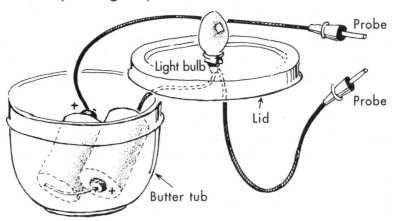

- Make a hole in the lid of the container. Put the bulb through the hole. (Make sure the hole is smaller than the diameter of the bulb's shank so that it will be held snugly.)

- Solder the wire end of one probe to the positive side of the battery. Solder the other probe to the bulb's threaded body shank. Solder the remaining wire to the negative end of the battery and to the tip of the bulb. (Soldering is necessary to maintain good connections for the electricity. When soldering, use the minimum of heat from your soldering iron to form the connections.

Excessive heat will destroy the bulb. While soldering is not difficult, you may wish to make a few practice runs before tackling the final connections.)

- After assembling your apparatus, test it. The bulb will light when the two probes are touched together if all your connections are proper. Now you can construct your question-and-answer cards.

The Question-and-Answer Cards

- Punch two columns of holes in the front of a file folder, one hole for each question and one hole for each answer. (See illustration)

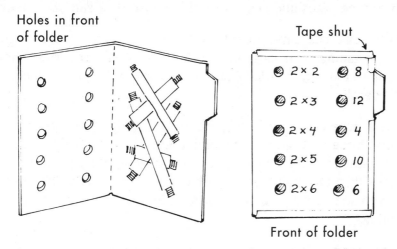

Holes in front of folder

Tape shut

2 × 2	8
2 × 3	12
2 × 4	4
2 × 5	10
2 × 6	6

Front of folder

- On the front of a folder, write one question next to each hole in the first column. Write one answer next to each hole in the second column.

- Cut aluminum foil into thin strips $\frac{1}{8}$ to $\frac{1}{4}$-inch wide. Each strip should be stretched from the question to the correct answer and fastened with tape. (Plot the location of questions and answers in advance, staggering the location of questions and answers to avoid a set pattern of responses.)

- Crossing aluminum strips one over the other will establish a multiplicity of responses. Unless this is desired, you must insulate any crossovers by placing a strip of masking tape over the bottom aluminum strip. (Tape the entire strip to make sure the patterns can't be seen by holding the card up to the light.)

- Cover each aluminum foil strip with masking tape up to the exposed holes.

- Prepare a file cabinet full of question-and-answer cards. Let the students help themselves to this approach to individualized instruction. Make cards for all areas of the curriculum. Have the students make their own remediation cards.

Constructing Box-Board Buildings

Single-, bi-, and tri-wall cardboard can be used in many building projects for your classroom. Cardboard can be glued, nailed, pegged, taped, tied, or slotted together for sturdiness.

* Make a simple table or stool by notching two pieces of cardboard into an X for the base and then cutting an additional piece for the top surface. Sizes and shapes can be adjusted to suit your needs.

* Construct three-dimensional rectangular or cubic blocks by gluing, stapling, taping, or nailing six pieces of cardboard together. They can be painted in bright colors, taped with colorful tape, or decorated with decals.

* Make a large cardboard box garden by cutting off the ends of several boxes and gluing or taping them together. The box can be lined with large plastic sheets, such as a heavy-duty painter's dropcloth, a tarpaulin, or even plastic trash bags. Then fill the box $\frac{3}{4}$ full with soil. Now you have a garden in your room ready for planting.

* Create puzzles from single pieces of cardboard glued together or from bi- or tri-wall cardboard. Shapes, numbers, and letters can be cut out with a jigsaw and decorated by painting or coloring.

* Appliance boxes and fiber barrels make excellent study carrels or private areas.

* Cardboard boxes can be stacked for good bookshelves.

* Cardboard boxes can be cut up to make banjos and kites.

* Try building with cardboard tubes—make chairs, tables, shelves, flashlights, telescopes, and cameras.

Good sources of tri-wall cardboard, along with cardboard carpentry ideas, are:

Building with Cardboard
Education Development Center
55 Chapel Street
Newton, MA 02160

Tri-Wall Containers, Inc.
100 Crossways Park West
Woodbury, NY 11797

Children enjoy bringing animals into the classroom. Homes for animals can be quite expensive if you purchase them commercially. Here are many ideas for animal homes that can be constructed from scrap or materials obtained at a minimal cost. Most important, children can build these homes with very little supervision. Try making some for your classroom.

> **WARNING:** Except for insects and worms, animals from the wild should not be brought into the classroom. Pet animals should be handled carefully.

Ant Homes

* Ant homes are also excellent for studying mealworms, pill bugs, caterpillars, roaches, earthworms, and ladybugs.

Materials: 3 clear plastic food containers or sandwich boxes; soil; glass and plastic tubing; drill for making holes; sponge; sugar

* Drill a hole (slightly smaller in diameter than the plastic tubing) at the ends of each of the 3 containers and connect them in a row with pieces of plastic tubing. The holes in the end boxes can be used for ventilation. (Fit these holes with a piece of glass tubing drawn out to a narrow tip so that the air gets in but the ants don't get out.)

* The simplest way to move an ant colony in is to take a section directly from an anthill and transfer it to the middle plastic container. (An alternative method is to place the colony in a jar covered by a piece of cloth held tight by a rubber band. Make a hole in the cloth, insert a piece of plastic tubing, and extend the other end of the tubing into the middle plastic container. Place the jar in water heated to 80 or 85° F. The ants will move through the tubing to the plastic container.)

Activity Ideas

* Put soil and a damp sponge in each of the outer two containers. Place some sugar in the first container and observe the activity.

* Try to find out what type of food ants like best. Place different foods in the outer two containers. Remember to keep the damp sponge in both containers with the food.

* Place 2 different ant species in the home, one in each outer container. Place food in the middle container.

* Other investigations can include whether ants prefer sand or dirt for homes; what temperature they prefer; their reactions to light.

Insect Homes

 Build insect homes from Popsicle sticks or tongue depressors that have been glued together. You can cover the sticks with screening to keep the insects in the home or you can put the Popsicle frame inside an old nylon stocking.

Bird Homes

 Make bird homes to hang in trees outside home or school from bleach bottles (thoroughly cleaned), gourds, coconut shells, and gallon or half-gallon milk cartons.

Egg Homes

Materials: Styrofoam cooler; aluminum pan; lamp cord; sheet of $\frac{1}{2}$-inch wire mesh; thermostat (available at farm stores or science supply houses); thermometer; 40-watt lightbulb; light socket; sheet of glass 20 x 25 cm; electrical tape; fertilized eggs from a hatchery

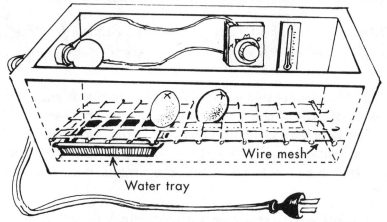

Egg home assembled (without top)

 Cut an opening at the bottom of the end of the cooler (through which you can change or fill the water pan). Next, cut a hole for the light socket at the top of the same end. Cut a rectangle in the lid of the cooler approximately 3 cm smaller than the sheet of glass. Tape the glass in place.

 Split the lamp cord close to the lightbulb and wire it to the thermostat. Tape carefully with electrical tape and tape the wires to the side of the cooler. Now connect the lamp cord to the socket.

 Place the water pan in the bottom of the cooler. Place a wire mesh floor about halfway down in the cooler. Check to be sure that it is secure. Tape the thermometer to the side of the cooler and adjust the thermostat so that the lightbulb turns off at 100° F.

 Place the eggs in the incubator. Remember to turn the eggs twice daily (put an X on one side of each egg to keep track), and keep the water pan filled.

Hummingbird Feeder

Materials: 20-dram clear prescription vial (from drugstore); ice pick or nail; thread or fine wire; tape; hummingbird food or sugar and red food coloring to make your own

WARNING: Do not breathe the fumes generated by the melting plastic.

* Use the heated ice pick or nail to punch a pair of holes on opposite sides of the plastic vial nail near its open end. (These holes should be extremely small so that insects are kept out and the liquid kept in.) Make sure that the holes are very close to, but not covered by, the bottom of the cap when the cap is in place.

* To make a hanger for the feeder, use thread or fine wire and secure the ends of the thread or wire with tape. For extra holding power, fold the ends of the thread back over the tape and wrap a second piece of tape around the vial.

* The hummingbird food can be a commercial nectar mix of the granular type, or you can make up your own sugar solution. Stir 4 or 5 heaping teaspoons of granulated sugar into a cup of warm water. Add enough red food coloring to give the mixture a scarlet hue.

* To fill the finished feeder, take off the cap and hold the vial upright. Fill with nectar, cap the container tightly, and quickly invert the tube (so that the feeding holes are at the bottom). Initially, a small amount of liquid may leak out of the feeding holes, but the leakage will stop as a vacuum is created inside the vial.

* Hang the feeder in the shade, near flowers.

Earthworm Behavior House

Materials: 2 pieces of 30 x 30-cm wood board; 2 pieces of 15 x 15-cm wood board; 1 piece of 30 x 30-cm glass; leaves of vegetables or dried leaves; loamy soil; earthworms

* Make a box 30 cm x 30 cm x 15 cm with a glass front. Fill the box nearly to the top with successive layers of loam, pressing down each layer before adding the next.

* Place lettuce leaves, dead leaves, or carrots on the surface of the soil, together with some worms. Keep the contents damp and study the behavior of the worms.

Related activities: BIS 10, BIS 18, BIS 30, SS 4

Making a Root Observation Chamber

When students observe how plants grow, it can be interesting to observe, measure, and infer how the roots as well as the stems and leaves show their growth.

Materials: plate glass with beveled edges (glass company can bevel edges) OR Plexiglas—3 sheets of 15 x 60 cm, 2 sheets of 7.5 x 15 cm, and one sheet of 7.5 x 60 cm; silicone caulking; soil; seeds; optional: 1-inch thick boards for a holder

* Assemble the glass observation chamber with silicone caulk. Make a 1.5-cm overlap where the front and back sections join the base. You can make a holder from 1-inch thick wood boards cut to 60-cm lengths and nailed to a base.

* Check the chamber for leaks by filling it with water. Drain and let it set for 24 hours. Then, fill it halfway with soil and plant some seeds.

* Once the seeds have germinated, you will be able to observe the root growth, its branching, and its rate of growth.

* Use your root observation chamber to show the movement of water through various kinds of soil. Place these layers from bottom to top in the chamber—gravel, sand, soil. The students can observe how water builds up before it can move from one layer to another.

Related activities: BIS 2, BIS 21, BIS 24, BIS 43

Constructing Circuit Boards

Materials: two 12 x 18-cm pieces of pegboard or cardboard, shoeboxes, or manila folders; brass paper fasteners; solder or masking tape; soldering iron; bell wire or paper clips or aluminum foil; flashlight bulb; batteries; masking tape

* First, make a sketch of the circuit you want to make. Put brass paper fasteners into each terminal hole. Turn the board over. Solder one end of a precut wire, with the insulation removed from each end, to two of the terminals to make a circuit. (See page 139 for an example.)

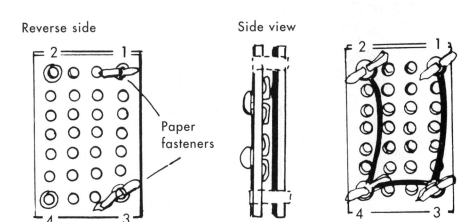

Reverse side   Side view

Paper fasteners

- Check your soldering job by turning the pegboard panel over and checking to see if a lightbulb lights when the wires are touched to the terminals. Make other circuits. When your circuit board is wired to your satisfaction, use a matching piece of pegboard as a backing, taping it with masking or similar tape.

- Make a variety of differently wired circuit boards.

- Use the circuit boards for students to infer wiring diagrams. For example, if you made a circuit between 1 and 3, when students touch terminals 1 and 3 with a lightbulb probe, the lightbulb will light.

Building a DeKro Water Treatment Plant

SS **9**

Water treatment plants remove materials from water. They remove floating solids (wood, leaves, rubbish) with screening and large nonfloating solids such as silt with a settling basin. Treatment plants remove suspended solids with filtration, dissolved chemicals and discoloration with alum, bacteria with chlorine, and dissolved gases with carbon. You can illustrate how a water treatment plant operates by building a model of the DeKro water treatment plant.

Materials: 6 square plastic containers; four $1\frac{1}{2}$-inch pinch clamps; 60 cm of 7-mm glass tubing; 30 cm of rubber tubing; 1 glass chimney; charcoal bits; 10 g of alum; chlorine bleach; wire mesh window screen; scrap lumber; gravel; coarse sand; fine sand; 2 baffle plates (from stores that sell replacement pads for humidifiers)

WARNING: This water is not for drinking!

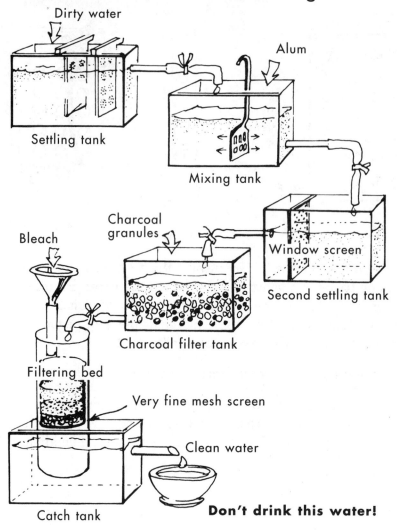

Dirty water

Settling tank

Alum

Mixing tank

Bleach

Charcoal
granules

Window screen

Second settling tank

Charcoal filter tank

Filtering bed

Very fine mesh screen

Clean water

Catch tank

Don't drink this water!

- Follow the diagram to construct the treatment plant.

- Use scrap lumber to support the 7 levels for a gravity flow.

- Dirty water goes into the settling tank, where large nonfloating solids settle to the bottom and floating solids are screened out.

- Alum is added in the mixing tank to neutralize dissolved chemicals. Stir to mix thoroughly.

- Settling tank with screening filters fine solids.

- Then a charcoal filter removes dissolved gases.

- Chlorine bleach is added to kill microbes as the water passes through the filtering bed, which consists of pebbles, coarse sand, and fine sand, in that order.

- The "treated" water goes into the catch tank and comes out "clean."

Related activities: BIS 47, BIS 48

Making Hardened-Flour Shapes SS 10

Materials: 4 cups flour; 1 cup salt; $1\frac{1}{2}$ cups water; hairpins or paper clips; cookie sheet; oven; tempera or acrylic paints; varnish

- Mix all ingredients together thoroughly and knead for 5 minutes. Use your hands, kitchen utensils, or cookie cutters to shape and form figures.

- Insert hairpins or paper clips in the back if you want to hang the shapes up or make them react to a magnet.

- Place the shapes on a cookie sheet and bake in a preheated oven at 350° F for 30 minutes to 1 hour.

- The shapes may then be painted in bright colors with tempera or acrylic paints. Protect this finish with a coat of varnish after drying.

- Hardened-flour shapes can be used for making geometric shapes, animal shapes, making circles with numbers embedded in them, weighing activities, symmetry lessons, classifying and sorting, and observation and inferring activities.

Related activities: BIS 16, BIS 27, BIS 42

Building a Foucault Pendulum SS 11

One of the most convincing proofs of the earth's rotation was first demonstrated in 1851 by the French physicist Jean Bernard Leon Foucault. Foucault hung a cannonball on a 219-foot wire attached to the dome of the Pantheon building in Paris.

The cannonball hung suspended almost to the floor. Thus suspended, the cannonball made a giant pendulum, free to swing in any direction. A pointer attached to the cannonball reached down into sand on the floor. When Foucault's pendulum was set in motion, the pointer traced a path in the sand below.

A pendulum set in motion in one direction will continue to move in the same direction. Foucault set the giant pendulum in motion in a north-south direction. As time passed, the pendulum appeared to shift the course of its motion in a clockwise direction.

Actually, the pendulum continued to move in the original north-south direction. It was the earth beneath the pendulum that was turning on its axis in a counterclockwise direction, causing the pointer on the cannonball to form clockwise tracings in the sand. This was convincing proof of the earth's rotation.

You can build a Foucault pendulum to demonstrate the physicist's experiment.

Materials: phonograph; pencil; jar; string; lead fishing sinker

◉ Set up the apparatus as shown in the illustration. Start the weight swinging. Turn the phonograph turntable to its slowest speed.

Related activities: BIS 41, BIS 94, SS 2

SS 12   *Weather or Not—Studying Weather*

Weather is a topic of universal concern and interest. Students of all ages are aware of and affected by the weather. At the middle and intermediate levels, interest spans greater periods of time, allowing for a more in-depth study of weather.

Weather stations may be constructed and maintained, data recorded, and inferences and predictions made. Generally, a study of weather involves observing and recording temperatures, humidity, and wind speeds and directions.

Measuring Wind Speed

Wind speed is measured by an anemometer.

Materials: scrap wood; two 50-cm wood dowels; one 25-cm dowel; plastic (to make cups); drill; 2 flat washers; plastic bead (to fit over 25-cm dowel); paint

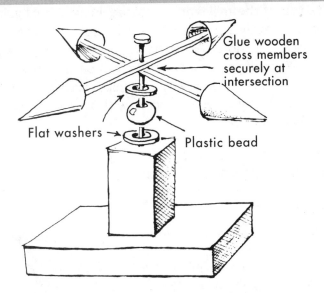

Glue wooden cross members securely at intersection

Flat washers →

Plastic bead

- Attach the 25-cm dowel to a heavy wood base. (If it is not securely anchored, it will topple in a strong wind.) At the top of the dowel, attach two 50-cm dowels at right angles to each other.

- At the ends of these dowels, attach plastic cups to catch the wind. One of the plastic cups should be painted a different color to keep track of one full revolution of the anemometer.

Finding Wind Direction

Materials: empty quart milk carton; plaster of Paris; wood dowel; small block of wood; small stones; drill; stapler; stiff cardboard; shellac or silicone

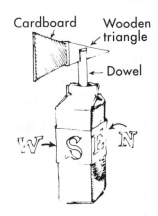

Cardboard   Wooden triangle

Dowel

W   S   E   N

- Fill the milk carton with plaster of Paris. When pouring the mixture into the container, add some small stones. (This will save on the amount of plaster needed and provide ballast for the carton.) Before the plaster hardens, insert the dowel into the mixture, centering it and making sure it is perpendicular. This is extremely important. Allow this mixture to harden completely.

- Staple the top of the milk carton closed. Make a triangular piece of wood approximately 1 x 3 inches. Drill a hole $\frac{3}{4}$ of the way into the piece of wood. The hole should be large enough for the dowel to fit into. Glue a triangle cut from stiff cardboard to the end of the wood triangle. Mark each side of the milk carton—North, South, East, and West. Spray the entire vane with shellac or silicone to protect it from the weather.

- Place the wind vane outdoors, orienting North on the milk carton in the direction of geographic north.

Measuring Humidity

You can observe changes in humidity with a hair hygrometer.

Materials: few strands of human hair; detergent; 50-g weight; rubber band; toothpick; scrap wood

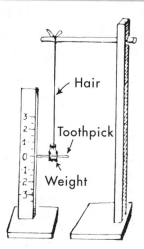

- Construct a stand and a scale marked with a zero point and graduations above and below zero. (See illustration above.) Wash the hair in detergent to remove oils. Attach one hair to the upper end of the stand and stretch it by attaching it to a 50-g weight.

- Use the rubber band to attach the toothpick to the weight so that it can serve as a pointer. Be sure that the pointer points exactly to zero on the scale.

- Changes in humidity will either shorten or lengthen the strand of hair. The changes will be reflected in readings above and below zero. Check with your local weather station and correlate your measurements with theirs. (This will let you adjust your scale so that it gives more accurate readings.)

Determining Relative Humidity

A wet- and dry-bulb thermometer is useful in determining relative humidity.

Materials: 2 thermometers; board; sock or muslin sleeve; small jar or test tube; water

* Attach two thermometers to a board. Leave one thermometer unchanged. This is the dry-bulb thermometer.

* Wrap the second thermometer in a sock or sleeve of muslin that fits snugly over the bulb of the thermometer. Suspend it in a small jar or test tube filled with water. Fasten the jar or test tube to the board so that its top is at the same level or slightly lower than the top of the thermometer bulb. Through capillary action, this bulb remains wet. This is the wet-bulb thermometer.

* Since evaporation is a cooling process, the wet-bulb thermometer should read lower than the dry-bulb thermometer. In order to determine the relative humidity, consult a relative humidity table. Two readings are needed, one from the dry and one from the wet-bulb thermometer.

Measuring Rainfall

Materials: steep-sided funnel; bottle; graduated cylinder; ruler

* Bury the bottle in a hole so that the funnel is just above the ground. (This prevents the bottle from tipping over and makes it easy to remove.)

* After a rain, pour the contents of the bottle into a graduated cylinder to determine the exact volume of rainwater collected. Measure the diameter of the top of the funnel. Also determine the surface area of the top of the funnel (Surface Area = πr^2).

* Knowing these and the amount of collected rain, you can determine the amount of rain per unit of area. If you have recorded the time period of the rainfall, you can calculate the rainfall per unit of area, per unit of time.

With these weather instruments, much data can be collected and plotted on graphs providing opportunities for many interpretations as well as correlations among various weather factors.

Related activities: BIS 38, BIS 46

Making a Kaleidoscope

Rotated reflections of different materials such as colored beads, pieces of colored paper, yarn, or ribbon alters their shape and color combinations into beautiful multiple images.

Materials: 3 same-size rectangular mirrors; rubber bands; tape; metal container (coffee, soup, or peanut can); 4 beads or marbles; clear rigid plastic sheet; colored plastic shards or bits of colored ribbon or yarn

- Tape the 3 mirrors together to form a triangle, with mirror surfaces facing inward. Wrap several rubber bands around the mirrors for reinforcement.

- Invert a can and place 4 beads or marbles in the circular groove on the container bottom. Place a piece of the plastic sheet on top. (The beads or marbles act as ball bearings and allow the plastic sheet to rotate smoothly.) Place the triangular-mirror tube upright on the plastic sheet. Insert small pieces of colored plastic shards, colored ribbon, or yarn in the triangular mirrored tube.

- To use the kaleidoscope look down into the triangular tube and gently rotate the plastic sheet.

Related activities: BIS 47, BIS 51, BIS 53

Making a Food-Tray Wave Tank

Materials: flat, plastic cafeteria tray; piece of Plexiglas (same size as the tray); drill; saber saw; silicone sealant; overhead projector; pencil; blocks of wood or paraffin; water.

- Drill a hole in the center of the tray for the saber saw to fit in.

- Then cut out the center of the tray with a saber saw. Leave a 6-cm border around the edge. Glue the Plexiglas to the tray with sealant.

- Place your completed wave tank on an overhead projector and add water. **WARNING: Be careful when using the wave tank. Do not let the water spill onto the projector.**

- Use a pencil point as a wave generator and blocks of wood or paraffin as barriers.

Related activities: BIS 14, BIS 67, BIS 83

Materials: constellation wheel and frame (page 148 and 149); cardboard; glue; brass fastener

* Glue the constellation wheel to a piece of cardboard. Then cut it out on the solid lines.

* Cut out the constellation frame on the solid and dashed lines. Also cut out the shaded areas. Then tape or glue the four corners of the frame to a piece of cardboard.

* Slip the wheel between the cardboard and the frame. Line it up so that the months on the constellation wheel show through the slits on the frame below N, W, S, and E.

* Then fasten the wheel to the cardboard with a brass fastener. Allow enough room for the wheel to rotate about the brass fastener. The brass fastener represents the North Star.

* To use your constellation finder, line up the month and day under North (the arrow above midnight). Go outside and hold the finder above your head with N pointing in the direction of geographical north. What you observe on the finder should be the same as what you observe in the sky.

Related activities: BIS 15, BIS 56, BIS 85

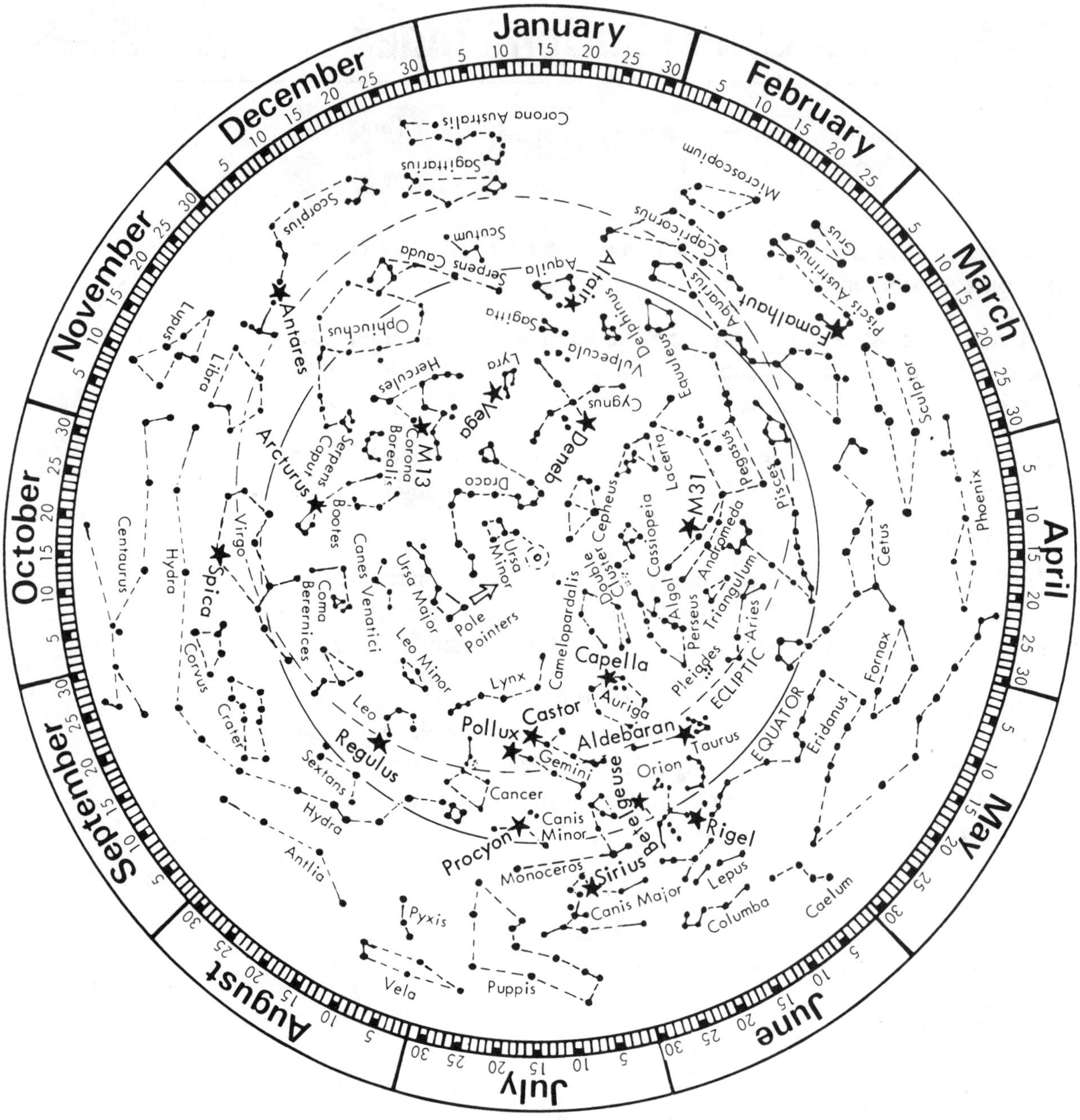
January
February
March
April
May
June
July
August
September
October
November
December
Corona Australis
Sagittarius
Scorpius
Scutum
Serpens Cauda
Aquila
Altair
Microscopium
Capricornus
Grus
Piscis Austrinus
Fomalhaut
Aquarius
Delphinus
Sagitta
Ophiuchus
Antares
Lupus
Libra
Hercules
Lyra
Vega
Vulpecula
Cygnus
Deneb
Equuleus
Sculptor
Phoenix
Serpens Caput
Corona Borealis
M13
Draco
Lacerta
Pegasus
Pisces
Arcturus
Bootes
Ursa Minor
Cepheus
Cassiopeia
M31
Andromeda
Cetus
Centaurus
Hydra
Virgo
Spica
Canes Venatici
Coma Berenices
Ursa Major
Pole Pointers
Camelopardalis
Double Cluster
Algol
Perseus
Triangulum
Aries
Corvus
Crater
Leo Minor
Lynx
Capella
Auriga
Pleiades
ECLIPTIC
Fornax
Eridanus
EQUATOR
Leo
Regulus
Sextans
Pollux
Castor
Gemini
Aldebaran
Taurus
Orion
Cancer
Hydra
Antlia
Procyon
Canis Minor
Betelgeuse
Rigel
Sirius
Monoceros
Canis Major
Lepus
Columba
Caelum
Pyxis
Vela
Puppis

star map

N

W

S

E

midnight
11 pm
1 am
10 pm
9 pm
8 pm
7 pm
2 am
6 pm
3 am
5 pm
4 am
4 pm
5 am
3 pm
6 am
2 pm
7 am
1 pm
8 am
noon
9 am
11 am
10 am

○

149

Preserving with Plastic

Materials: plastic resin with hardener (a catalyst available at auto supply or hobby stores); mineral oil; wooden stirrers; paper containers; plastic measuring cup; plastic molds (small or large ones can be used); tweezers; fan (for ventilation); newspapers to work on; thermometer; objects to embed in the plastic; toothpicks; file or sandpaper

WARNING: **The resin and hardener used in this activity are dangerous. It should be done only under the direct supervision of the teacher. Make sure that all the safety precautions on all containers are read and followed and that all windows in the classroom are open, or conduct the activity outdoors.**

- Assemble the equipment and materials. Make sure the plastic molds are at least 65° F or warmer.

- In a paper container, add hardener (catalyst) to the resin, using the proportional amounts indicated in the directions on the label.

- Coat the plastic mold with a very light layer of mineral oil.

- Decide on what you want to embed in the plastic. Almost anything will work: mealworms in stages from larvae to adult beetle, biological specimens, minerals, and so forth. Remember, however, that the result is permanent.

- Pour the resin into the cavities of the plastic mold until the bottom is covered (about $\frac{1}{8}$-inch deep). Allow it to stand until the plastic has gelled (about 15 to 20 minutes). Check for solidity with a toothpick.

- After the first layer has gelled, pour a second layer ($\frac{1}{8}$ to $\frac{1}{4}$-inch thick), using slightly less hardener.

- Use tweezers to dip the object to be embedded into the paper container of catalyzed resin. Then place the embedded object into the liquid resin in the mold. (The first pour was the top layer of the finished item; thus, you should position your object upside down.)

- Allow the second layer to cure until gelled, usually 4 to 5 hours. When the layer is completely hardened, remove the casting from the mold. Do not pry the casting out or it may be damaged.

- Sand or file the back of the casting until smooth. Allow it to dry completely 24 hours before using.

Constructing Salt and Flour Relief Maps

SS **17**

Materials: salt; flour; watercolor paints; brush; piece of heavy cardboard; container to mix ingredients; water; map (optional)

* Combine 3 parts salt, 1 part flour, and enough water to bring the solution to the consistency of dough. The thickness of the material may be modified by varying the amount of water. (Other recipes that can be used for this activity appear in CSR 9 and CSR 10.)

* Draw a map outline on the cardboard. Then, cover the cardboard with a thin film of the salt and flour mixture.

* Depending on the map features you wish to include, you can add more salt and flour mixture after the first application has dried. Add colors to show rivers, mountains, and so forth if you wish.

* You can press objects such as train tracks and footprints into the wet mixture.

* Among other features that might be included are counties, countries, lakes, rivers, cities, highways, and points of interest.

* Students may want to construct maps of their own communities using the salt and flour mixture.

Related activities: BIS 56, SS 3

Inverting an Image—Using a Pinhole Camera

SS **18**

A pinhole camera is a good way to demonstrate the fact that light travels in a straight line unless it is interrupted by something placed in its path. Most cameras interrupt and converge light rays by the use of one or more lenses placed in the light's path. The pinhole camera does not use a lens; instead, it uses a very small pinhole.

Materials: small cardboard box; black spray paint; aluminum foil; sharp needle; wax paper; candle

* Spray paint the entire interior of a box with black paint. Let this dry thoroughly. In the center of one end of the box, cut an opening about 2 inches square.

- Cover the opening with a piece of unwrinkled aluminum foil. With the needle puncture a tiny hole in the middle of the foil. In the center of the opposite end of the box, cut an opening about 3 to 4 inches square. Cover the opening with a piece of wax paper.

- Darken the room and point the pinhole end of the camera at a lighted candle positioned about 6 inches away from you. View the backside of your pinhole camera. A burning candle should be observed on the wax paper, but it will be an inverted image.

SS 19

Making a Periscope

A periscope can be used to illustrate reflected images.

Materials: quart-size empty milk container; two mirrors

- Cut a viewing opening near the bottom of one side of the milk carton. Cut another opening near the top on the opposite side. Arrange the mirrors at 45 degree angles to the horizontal base of the milk carton. The mirrors reflecting faces should face and be parallel to each other.

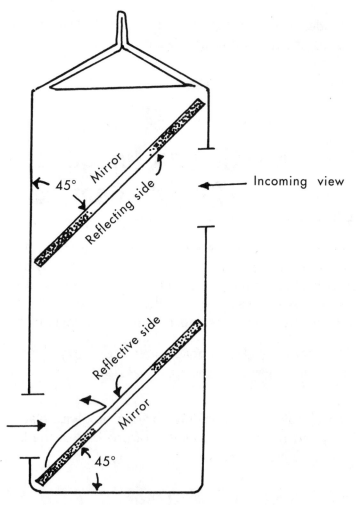

Building a Plant Light-Direction Box | SS **20**

Plants need light to grow into well-shaped healthy plants. They will seek ways to reach light.

> **Materials:** cardboard shoebox with cover; cardboard for baffles; scissors; plant

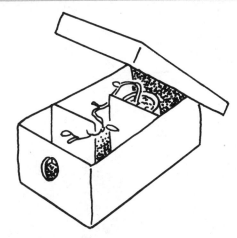

* Cut a hole in one end of the shoebox. Construct 2 light baffles in an interrupted path inside the shoebox so that light coming through the hole cannot follow a straight path. This is like a maze for light.

* Place a plant beyond the baffle farthest from the hole in the shoebox. Cover the box and place it near a window.

* Observe the direction of plant growth daily.

Making a Sundial | SS **21**

> **Materials:** stiff cardboard or wood; 2 protractors; $4\frac{1}{4}$-inch square sheet of paper; scissors; protractor

* Tape a protractor to the cardboard or wood.

* Construct a right-angle triangle from the $4\frac{1}{4}$-inch square sheet of paper (The triangle should have two $4\frac{1}{4}$ inch sides.) Draw a line $\frac{1}{4}$ inch up on the $4\frac{1}{4}$ inch sides. (See diagram.)

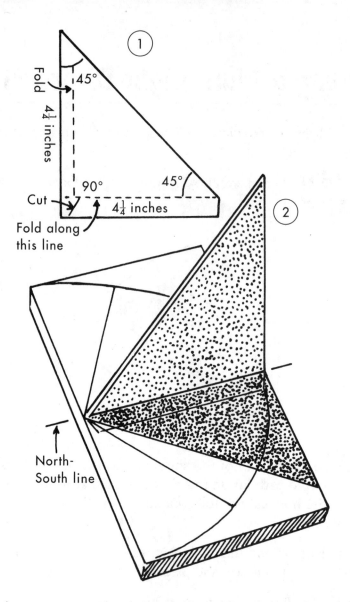

- Cut in $\frac{1}{4}$ inch on the line. Fold up and crease the paper along both $\frac{1}{4}$-inch base lines. With the triangle folded, make a cut along the crease line. Stop $\frac{1}{2}$-inch short of cutting all the way through.

- Slip the flat pads (the folded-over sections of the triangle) under the protractor. Tape the protractor down at that point where the flat pads go under the protractor. The triangle should stand upright.

- Position the sundial so that the triangle aligns in a north-south line. Record the position of the shadow formed by the triangle. Do this every hour. Correlate the shadow angles with current clock readings. Once this is done, the sundial becomes your timepiece.

CREATIVE SCIENCING RECIPES

Every Recipe You've Always Wanted But Couldn't Locate

Creative sciencing recipes are designed to provide you with sources of basic materials such as paints, inks, dyes, pastes, clays, papier-mâché, modeling materials, and nature recipes. They also give you instructions for manufacturing gases, making a stethoscope, constructing a manometer, preparing a bubble solution, and making your own slides.

The recipes are not technical; they are easy to prepare and call for inexpensive ingredients that are readily obtained. We have purposely avoided lengthy applications statements since all these recipes have a variety of uses. The limitations for their use will be dictated by your individual needs. Most of the recipes can be prepared by your students.

Powder Paint

BASIC POWDER PAINT

5 T powder paint

5 T water

liquid starch or detergent

Put powder paint and water in an empty and washed school milk carton. Press the lid down firmly and shake the carton until the paint is thoroughly mixed. So that the paint keeps and goes on more smoothly, add enough liquid starch or detergent to give it the consistency of cream or poster paint.

LARGE QUANTITY RECIPE

8 T powder paint

1 t white library paste

2 T liquid starch

oil of cloves, wintergreen, or peppermint

Mix the first 3 ingredients and add enough water to give the mixture a consistency of cream or poster paints. To prevent a sour smell, add a little oil of cloves, wintergreen, or peppermint.

WATERCOLOR

For a transparent watercolor, add sufficient water to the powder paint to obtain a runny consistency. For an opaque watercolor, add enough water or liquid starch to the powder paint to make a creamy consistency.

COLORED INK

Mix enough water with the powder paint to allow it to flow easily from a lettering pen or mechanical drawing tool.

OIL PAINT

Mix 2 tablespoons of powder paint with water to allow it to flow easily from a brush, lettering pen, or mechanical drawing tool.

Add a few drops of glycerin and powder paint to raw linseed oil to make a thick cream consistency. Use zinc oxide with linseed oil for a white oil paint.

(Alternative: Add boiled linseed oil to powder paint and stir well.)

ENAMEL

Add clear shellac, lacquer, or varnish to the powder paint until you reach a desired brushing consistency.

WOOD STAIN

Mix powder paint with linseed oil or turpentine until you reach a brushing consistency. To make a waterproof lacquer, mix powder paint with a gloss oil. Rub crayons along the grain of the wood to be stained. Then rub the wood vigorously with a cloth saturated in linseed oil.

Finger Paint

CSR **2**

CORNSTARCH FINGER PAINT

$\frac{1}{2}$ cup cornstarch

1 quart boiling water

2 T glycerin (optional) to keep paint from drying

oil of cloves or wintergreen

poster paint, India ink, or powdered tempera

Dissolve the starch in a small amount of cold water and gradually add the boiling water. Cook until clear. Add 2 tablespoons of glycerin. Add oil of cloves or wintergreen (to keep the paint from souring). For color, use poster paint, India ink, or powdered tempera mixed with water to the consistency of a smooth paste.

LIQUID STARCH FINGER PAINT

1 T liquid starch

colored powder paint

2 T glycerin (optional)

sheet of dampened paper

Pour a tablespoon of liquid starch in the center of a sheet of dampened paper. Add a small amount of colored powder paint. Work the powder paint and starch together.

LAUNDRY STARCH FINGER PAINT

2 quarts boiling water

1 cup soap flakes

1 cup laundry starch

$\frac{1}{2}$ cup talcum powder

2 T glycerin (optional)

Dilute the starch in a cup of cold water. Add the boiling water slowly, stirring constantly to avoid lumping. Stir in the soap flakes and talcum powder. (This paint can be used to finger paint on glass or over a heavy coat of crayons.) Yield: 5 pints.

FLOUR FINGER PAINT

2 cups flour

1 cup sugar

1 cup cornstarch

cold water

boiling water

2 T glycerin (optional)

Mix the ingredients in cold water to a thick, heavy paste. Pour in enough boiling water to make a thick, heavy paste, stirring constantly until clear.

CHALK FINGER PAINT

colored chalk (finely ground)

water

school paste

2 drops of oil of cloves

2 T glycerin (optional)

Mix chalk with water, school paste, and 2 drops of oil of cloves. (This paint has an interesting texture.)

CSR 3

Printing Ink

OIL-BASED PRINTING INK

2 quarts powder paint

1 part linseed oil

1 part varnish

Mix the ingredients to the consistency of a smooth paste. This ink spreads on evenly but will not dry quickly. It is good for paper with a rough-textured surface.

VARNISH-BASED INK

> 3 parts powder paint
>
> 1 part varnish

Mix the powder paint and varnish with a palette knife on glass. Use a brayer, or printing roller, to roll the mixture back and forth until it is tacky before applying it to the block to be printed. This ink will dry more quickly than the oil-based ink and is suitable for use on nonabsorbent, smooth-finish paper. (The ink can be thinned with denatured alcohol.)

Bleaching and Dyeing

CSR 4

BLEACHED FLOUR AND SUGAR SACKS

> chloride of lime (bleaching powder)
>
> water
>
> 5% sulfuric acid
>
> carbonate of soda
>
> naptha soap
>
> kerosene

Make a strong solution of water and chloride of lime. Allow it to settle and then draw off the clear liquid. Rinse the sacks in clean water mixed with the 5% sulfuric acid. **(WARNING: Acid should be added to water; never add water to acid!)** Then pull the sacks slowly through the bleaching solution.

Rinse the sacks well in water containing a little carbonate of soda. If any color remains, allow the fabric to stay a short time in the sulfuric acid solution. Be sure to rinse well.

Soak the sacks in tepid water. Wash them well with naphtha soap, roll them tightly, and dampen them with kerosene. Allow them to stand overnight. Then wash out and boil the sacks with a bleaching powder or naphtha soap. If the color remains, the process should be repeated.

(Alternative—Use a commercial bleach, following directions carefully.)

NATURAL DYES

Collect plants, moss, herbs, roots, nuts, berries, and so on. Chop a quantity of one of these materials and put it through a meat grinder. Cover the ground material with water and allow it to stand overnight. Drain off the water the next morning and save it. Add a little more water to the pulp and simmer for 30 minutes.

After allowing the pulp to simmer, drain off the water and add it to the water drained from the ground material. Add more water to cover the fabric if necessary.

Rinse the dried fabric in hot water, wring it well, and then place it in the dye, making sure it is well-covered.

Bring the dye to a simmering stage and cook until the fabric is as deep in color as you wish. Rinse the fabric in lukewarm water. Squeeze lightly but do not wring. Avoid direct rays of sunlight while the fabric is drying.

CSR 5   Silk Screen Paint

TEMPERA SILK SCREEN PAINT

    tempera paint

    soap flakes

    water

Add a small quantity of soap flakes to the tempera to give it viscosity and to deter drying. Add water only if necessary. If the paint is too thick, it will clog the screen. If too thin, it will run. Finger paint of a creamy consistency can be used instead of tempera.

LIQUID STARCH SILK SCREEN PAINT

    liquid starch

    powder paint

Add liquid starch to powder paint and mix until it is the consistency of light paste.

Paste

BOILED FLOUR PASTE

$\frac{1}{2}$ cup flour

water

oil of wintergreen or peppermint

Add enough water to the flour to make a thin paste. Boil the paste for 5 minutes over low heat, stirring constantly. Cool and thin the paste with water. Add a few drops of wintergreen or peppermint to keep the paste from spoiling. Keep it in a covered jar and use it in any projects requiring large quantities of paste.

CORNSTARCH PASTE

2 T cornstarch

cold water

boiling water

Add enough cold water to the cornstarch to make a smooth paste. Add boiling water until the mixture turns clear. Cook until it thickens and then remove it from the heat. This paste becomes thicker as it cools. It may be thinned with water. Use cornstarch paste on tissue paper or thin cloth since it is less likely to show than flour paste.

WALLPAPER PASTE

1 cup wallpaper paste

water

oil of wintergreen, peppermint, or salicylic acid

Mix the wallpaper paste with water until the desired consistency is reached. Add a few drops of wintergreen, peppermint, or salicylic acid to keep the paste from souring. Store it in a jar.

BOOKMAKER'S PASTE

1 t flour

2 t cornstarch

$\frac{1}{4}$ t powdered alum

6 T water

Mix the first three ingredients together. Add the water slowly, stirring until smooth. Cook the mixture over low heat, preferably in a double boiler. Stir constantly until the paste is thickened. Keep it in airtight jars and thin with water when necessary. Use this paste to make notebooks and in bookmaking projects.

BOOK PASTE

> library paste
>
> hot water

Thin ordinary library paste with hot water to the consistency of very thick cream. This paste is excellent for mending books.

ADHESIVE PASTE

Mix equal parts of paste and glue. Use the adhesive paste when pasting objects too heavy to be held securely with regular paste on thick cardboard.

LAMINATING PASTE

Mix equal parts of glue and water. Use this paste to brush between the sheets when laminating paper with cellophane or other shiny surfaces.

CSR 7 # Clay

SELF-HARDENING CLAY

This clay hardens in drying and requires no baking. It can be bought commercially in craft stores or supply houses. It is practical to use when you have no kiln or when you do not wish to fire children's work. To make your own, add 1 part dextrin to 19 parts clay flour.

Dextrin added to clay will harden pieces so that they will be substantial enough to last without firing. Be sure to use dextrin made from yellow corn. (White dextrin is not satisfactory.)

Dextrin may also be worked into wet clay. Use a teaspoonful of dextrin to a pound of wet clay. Objects made from this clay may be painted when dry.

CREPE CLAY

> 1 sheet crepe paper (any color)
>
> 1 T salt
>
> 1 cup flour
>
> water

Mix the salt and flour. Cut the crepe paper into tiny pieces (confetti size). Place the pieces in a large bowl and add only enough water to cover the paper. Allow the mixture to soak for 15 minutes and pour off the excess water. Add enough of the flour-salt mixture to make a stiff dough. Knead it well until it is blended with the crepe paper.

FLOUR CLAY

> 1 cup flour
>
> 1 cup salt
>
> 1 t powdered alum
>
> water

Add water slowly to the flour, salt, and alum. Knead until it has a claylike consistency and then wrap in a wet cloth. It can keep for a few days. Flour clay can be used on maps to show relief and can be painted when dry. It keeps its shape without crumbling. For color, add powder paint to the water when mixing.

CORNSTARCH CLAY

> $\frac{1}{2}$ cup cornstarch
>
> 1 cup salt
>
> 1 cup boiling water

Boil the ingredients to a soft-ball stage and knead on wax paper until malleable. Wrap the clay in a wet cloth to keep it for a few days. Cornstarch clay may be pressed on maps to show relief, and when dry, it can be painted. It retains its shape without crumbling. For color, add powder paint to the water when mixing.

MAGNESITE MODELING CLAY

> magnesite (a building material)
>
> magnesium chloride

Mix magnesite with enough magnesium chloride to produce a doughlike consistency. Work with the magnesite dough on wax paper and use a rolling pin to flatten it like clay. Leave the material on the wax paper to dry. Use the clay to make beads and tiles. If the dough gets too sticky, dip the modeling tool you're using into water. (Tongue depressors and old table knives make good modeling tools.) Color with powder paint, varnish, or rub it with linseed oil when dry.

Papier Mâché

BASIC PULP

Tear newspapers, paper plates, or egg cartons into fine bits. Cover the paper bits with water and soak for 24 hours in a nonrusting container. Put the mixture in a cloth bag and squeeze it to get rid of excess water. Work on a wax-paper surface so that water will not damage the table or desk.

Add one of the following for each quart of pulp:

> 6 T flour
>
> 6 T dry laundry starch or 1 cup of cooked starch paste (Starch paste will not sour as readily as flour paste.)
>
> 1 cup liquid starch
>
> 1 cup thin library paste
>
> 1 cup wheat (wallpaper) paste mixed to consistency of cream
>
> 1 cup boiled flour paste (see CSR 6)

A few drops of wintergreen or oil of cloves will help to keep the pulp from souring. A little salt added to the mixture will prevent fermentation. Knead the pulp to the consistency of soft modeling clay. Drying may take as long as a week.

QUICK-DRYING AND MODELING PULP

> 4 cups papier mâché pulp
>
> 1 cup plaster of Paris
>
> $\frac{1}{2}$ t commercial glue

Combine the ingredients and knead to the consistency of heavy dough. It will dry in 3 to 6 hours.

For greater tensile strength, make modeling pulp by adding 1 cup of plaster of Paris to 1 gallon of any papier mâché pulp. Mix thoroughly. This pulp is suitable for modeling fruits, vegetables, toys, animals, and so on.

CSR 9   *Sawdust Modeling*

SAWDUST 1

> 2 cups sawdust (clean and fine)
>
> 1 cup flour
>
> 1 T glue
>
> hot water or liquid starch

Mix the sawdust, flour, and glue, and moisten with water or starch until it reaches a modeling consistency. If this sawdust mix is used to make ornaments, strings or wires should be put in place while they are being modeled. After drying, the ornaments may be painted.

SAWDUST 2

      sawdust

      wallpaper paste

      water

Mix equal parts of the ingredients. If the mixture is sticky, add more sawdust.

SAWDUST 3

      3 cups sawdust

      1 cup wheat paste

      water

Add enough water to mix the ingredients. Do not make the mixture too stiff.

SAWDUST 4

      1 cup sawdust

      1 cup plaster of Paris

      thin glue

Mix the ingredients. Add enough glue to hold the mixture together.

SAWDUST 5

      2 cups sawdust

      1 cup plaster of Paris

      $\frac{1}{2}$ cup wheat (or wallpaper) paste

      2 cups water

Mix the ingredients. Add water gradually until it reaches a modeling consistency. This sawdust mix is excellent for making puppet heads, fruits, vegetables, masks, figures, and animals.

SAWDUST 6

      1 cup sawdust

      water

Add enough water to mix the sawdust into a pliable pulp. The mixture will appear pebbled.

SAWDUST 7

1 cup flour

1 quart water

1 t alum

1 t oil of cloves

sawdust

Cook the flour and water until it reaches a creamy stage. Add alum. Remove the liquid from the stove and add cloves. Stir in enough sawdust to make a modeling consistency. This sawdust may be painted with powder paints or other coloring media when dry.

TEXTURE SAWDUST

sawdust

powder paint

water

Mix powder paint with water to a thin, creamy consistency. Pour the liquid over sawdust, stir well, and spread on a newspaper to dry. Use this sawdust mix to sprinkle on a glued surface for a textured effect.

SAWDUST MIX FOR RELIEF MAPS

Add a teaspoon of commercial glue to any of the sawdust recipes to increase the adhesive quality of the sawdust mix when applying it to a wood surface.

CSR **10**

Dough Modeling

DOUGH 1

2 cups flour

2 cups salt

water

Mix the flour and salt. Add enough water to make a creamy consistency. Powder paint or other coloring may be added, or the dough may be painted after it is dry. This dough is excellent for relief maps. Build the elevations in layers, allowing each to dry before adding another.

DOUGH 2

$\frac{1}{2}$ cup soft breadcrumbs

$\frac{1}{2}$ cup flour

$\frac{1}{2}$ t powdered alum

beaten egg white

Mix all the ingredients together and color with powder paint or watercolors.

DOUGH 3

1 cup flour

$\frac{1}{2}$ cup salt

3 t powdered alum

water

Add enough water to the other ingredients to make a proper consistency.

DOUGH 4

$\frac{1}{2}$ cup table salt

$\frac{1}{2}$ cup cornstarch

$\frac{1}{2}$ cup water

Mix the ingredients thoroughly and cook the mixture over low heat, stirring constantly until it stiffens into a lump. Use the dough as soon as it is cool enough to handle.

DOUGH 5

1 cup cornstarch

1 cup salt

1 cup cold water

Mix the ingredients and cook the mixture over low heat. Cool it and allow it to set until it does not stick to the fingers. A few drops of food coloring or powder paint may be added to the mixture for color.

This dough may be cut with cookie cutters or pressed into a butter mold. Holes for hanging may be punched with a toothpick before the material is dry. Glitter, sequins, or feathers may be pressed into the damp dough.

Nature Recipes

DRYING PLANTS FOR WINTER BOUQUETS

Strip the leaves from fresh flowers immediately. Tie the flowers by their stems with string and hang them with the heads down in a cool, dry place away from the light. Darkness is essential for preserving their color. Thorough drying takes about 2 weeks.

PRESERVING FALL LEAVES

Place alternate layers of powdered borax and leaves in a box, making sure leaves are completely covered. Allow them to stand for 4 days. Shake off the borax and wipe each leaf with liquid floor wax. Rub a warm iron over a cake of paraffin and then press the iron over the front and back of the leaves.

PRESERVING MAGNOLIA LEAVES

Mix two parts of water with one part of glycerin. Place stems with magnolia leaves in the mixture and let them stand for several days. The leaves will turn brown and will last many years. Their surfaces may be painted or sprayed with silver or gold paint.

KEEPING CATTAILS

Use cattails in their natural color or tint them by shaking metallic powders over them. Handle them carefully. Cattails are dry and fall apart easily.

TREATING GOURDS

Soak some gourds in water for two hours. Scrape them clean with a knife. Rub them with fine sandpaper and cut an opening to remove the seeds while the gourds are still damp.

PRESSING WILD FLOWERS

When gathering plant specimens, include the roots, leaves, flowers, and seed pods. Place them between newspapers, laying two blotters under the newspaper and two blotters on top to absorb the moisture. Place all the layers between two sheets of corrugated cardboard and press.

Change the newspapers three times during the week. It usually takes 7 to 10 days to press plant specimens. Cardboard covered with cotton batting makes a good mounting base. Lay each specimen on the cotton and cover with cellophane or plastic wrap to preserve their color.

MAKING INDIAN COLOR DYES

Seed pods, bark, leaves, and roots contain coloring that can be made into attractive dyes. Collect and process them, following the directions under the heading "Natural Dyes" in CSR 4.

You can get the following colors by processing one of the materials listed below. With some experimenting, you may be able to process other natural materials to get colors or combine some for new and unusual effects.

brown—walnut shells

red brown—onion leaves, bark

purple—blueberries, elderberries, grapes

yellow—mustard, sumac, peach leaves, moss

red—root and berry of the cactus

black—oak bark, gum of the piñon tree

Manufacturing Oxygen (O$_2$)   CSR 12

Pour an inch of hydrogen peroxide into a test tube and add a small amount of manganese dioxide. Shake slightly and notice the reaction taking place. Insert a glowing splint and observe what happens. (See BIS 39.)

Manufacturing Carbon Dioxide (CO$_2$)   CSR 13

See BIS 39 and BIS 84 before reading on. Then fill a collecting bottle with water and place it in a pan. Pour baking soda into the bottle, and when all preparations are made, add vinegar. The tube should be inserted into the water-filled collecting bottle. When the CO_2 has been collected, place a glass plate over the mouth of the bottle and remove it from the pan.

> **WARNING: Any gas built up in a closed system is a potential danger.**

Stethoscope

Small funnel

T-tube or Y-tube

rubber tubing

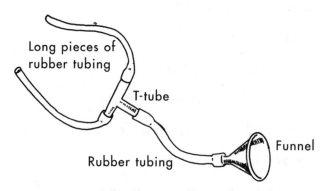

Long pieces of rubber tubing

T-tube

Rubber tubing

Funnel

Slip a piece of rubber tubing 7 or 8-cm long over the tip of the funnel. Insert the T-tube (or Y-tube) into the other end of a short piece of the rubber tubing. Attach longer pieces of tubing to both arms of the T-tube.

To use the stethoscope, have one student hold the funnel firmly over his or her heart while another listens to the heartbeat through the long tube.

An Instrument to Observe Heartbeats

manometer tube

thistle tube

colored water

wood base

plastic tube

masking tape

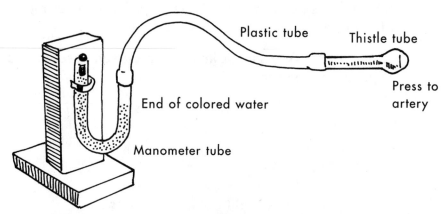

Plastic tube

Thistle tube

End of colored water

Press to artery

Manometer tube

Attach the manometer tube to the wood base with masking tape. Pour colored water into the tube until it is $\frac{1}{2}$ full. Attach one end of the plastic tube to the manometer. Attach the other end of a plastic tube to the thistle tube. (See page 170.)

Find the carotid artery in the neck, alongside the windpipe. Press the thistle tube against the region of the carotid artery. The column of water in the manometer tube should pulsate with each heartbeat.

Bubble Solution
CSR **16**

4 L tap water

240 ml liquid soap detergent

one 4-L container

wire bubble blowers

container for each student

Pour the soap into the water and stir gently to mix the two ingredients. Then invite the students to make bubbles.

Slide Pictures
CSR **17**

picture from magazine

clear contact paper

viewfinder below

Select a picture from a magazine. Cut out the viewfinder and place it on the image selected. Draw a pencil line around the image. Cut out the image just outside the guidelines. You should have a 2 x 2-inch square.

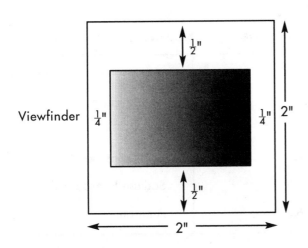

Take a piece of clear contact paper and peel off the paper backing. (Keep the backing for burnishing.) Press the printed surface of your picture onto the sticky side of the contact paper. Burnish the photograph carefully, image-side up. For added protection, place the paper backing on the photograph before you rub.

Soak the assembly in water for 2 minutes. Then peel away the paper with the printed image. Sponge away the milky residue and rinse the film well. Center the image and press the sticky side of the wet film onto a slide mount. Dry the mounted image and trim off the excess plastic.

CSR 18

The Universal Indicator— pH Measurement

Foods or other substances can be identified as acidic, neutral, or basic. Dyes used to identify these are called indicators. Another such indicator is the assessment of the pH level.

The term *pH* is an abbreviation for the hydrogen concentration of a solution obtained from foods or other substances. Based on the pH concentration, a solution can be identified as acidic, neutral, or basic.

The pH is determined by the use of Hydrion paper, which is a universal indicator. This paper changes color when it comes in contact with liquids obtained from specific foods or substances. Resultant colors correlate with various levels on the pH scale.

The colors representing the various pH levels are shown in a chart on the Hydrion paper container. You simply match the resultant color to the colors and the numerical pH values on the chart. The lower the numerical value, the more acidic the material is. The higher the number, the more basic or alkaline the material is.

pH Values (approximately) of Some Common Substances			
	pH Value		**pH Value**
Vinegar	2.5	Water (pure)	7.0
Cabbage	5.3	Borax	9.2
Lemon	2.3	Sodium carbonate	11.6
Cow's milk	6.5	Sodium bicarbonate	8.4
Flour, wheat	6.3	Ammonia	11.1

Substitutes for common chemicals to use in pH testing:

HOUSEHOLD ITEMS

White vinegar—acetic acid 5%

Nail polish remover—acetone

Alum—aluminum potassium sulfate

Household ammonia—ammonia hydroxide

Chalk—calcium carbonate

Light corn syrup—dextrose

Coffee filters—filter paper

Hydrogen peroxide—hydrogen peroxide (12% concentration)

Aspirin—salicylic acid

Baking soda—sodium bicarbonate

Table salt—sodium chloride

DRUGSTORE ITEMS

Boric acid

Ethyl alcohol

Glycerin

Epsom salts

Mineral oil

Sulfur

OTHERS

Lime (garden supply store)—calcium hydroxide

Copper sulfate (farm supply store)

Muriatic acid (hardware store)—hydrochloric acid

Tannic acid (boil oak bark in water)

Kali Matter

This solid has some unusual properties that fascinate students. Kali is great to use for making observations, formulating hypotheses, and making inferences.

$\frac{1}{4}$ cup liquid starch

$\frac{1}{2}$ cup white water-soluble glue

$\frac{1}{4}$ t salt

Mix the three ingredients together. If these proportions are too large, use any 1 to 2 ratio (starch to glue) and a pinch of salt.

APPENDIX A
CONTENTS by Skills and Subject Areas

This topical table of contents is designed to help you organize your science program around specific subjects and find ideas on how to reinforce general science skills your students need to practice. Reference to the National Science Education Standards (NSES) is also included, with page numbers of the NSES book, to refer to for science skills and subject areas.

APPENDIX B

Brainstorming in Science (BIS) Activities Classified by Related Subject Areas

Reading and Language Arts (24 activities):

3, 4, 5, 19, 20, 23, 27, 36, 38, 45, 50, 53, 55, 58, 59, 62, 64, 66, 69, 73, 77, 78, 84, 90

Math (37 activities):

1, 2, 7, 8, 9, 11, 12, 14, 16, 17, 18, 23, 29, 30, 31, 32, 35, 38, 42, 43, 45, 46, 49, 50, 53, 57, 58, 60, 61, 68, 70, 71, 72, 73, 80, 86, 90

Social Studies (17 activities):

10, 26, 30, 31, 44, 45, 50, 52, 53, 55, 62, 64, 66, 82, 84, 86, 90

Art (21 activities):

3, 4, 26, 29, 30, 42, 55, 57, 58, 64, 72, 76, 77, 78, 79, 80, 81, 84, 88, 89, 90

Music (4 activities):

13, 63, 72, 90

APPENDIX C

Where Do We Go from Here? Sources for More Ideas and Activities

Professional Associations and Government Organizations (with Web Sites Included)

American Solar Energy Society, 2400 Central Ave., Suite G-1, Boulder, CO 80301; (303) 443-3130 http://www.ases.org/solar

American Water Works Association, 6666 W. Quincy Ave., Denver, CO 80235; (303) 347-6140; (800) 926-7337 http://www.awwa.org

American Zoo and Aquarium Association, 7970-D Old Georgetown Rd., Bethesda, MD 20814; (301) 907-7777 http://www.aza.org

The Annenberg/CPB Math and Science Project, 901 E St., NW, Washington, DC 20004-2037; (202) 879-9654 http://www.learner.org

Association for Supervision and Curriculum Development (ASCD), 1250 N. Pitt St., Alexandria, VA 22314-1403; (703) 549-9110 http://www.ascd.org

Biological Sciences Curriculum Study (BSCS), 5415 Mark Dabling Blvd., Colorado Springs, CO 80918-3842; (719) 531-5550 http://www.bscs.org

Challenger Learning Centers, Challenger Center for Space Science Education, 1029 N. Royal St., Suite 300, Alexandria, VA 22314; (703) 683-9740 http://www.challenger.org

Council for Exceptional Children, 1920 Association Dr., Reston, VA 20191-1589; (703) 620-3660; (703) 264-9446 (TTY) http://www.cec.sped.org

Educational Development Center, 55 Chapel St., Newton, MA 02158-1060; (617) 969-7100 http://www.edc.org

Eisenhower National Clearinghouse for Mathematics and Science Education (ENC), The Ohio State University, 1929 Kenny Rd., Columbus, OH 43210-1079; (800) 621-5785; (614) 292-7784 http://www.enc.org

Environmental Action Coalition, 625 Broadway, 9th Floor, New York, NY 10012; (212) 677-1601

ERIC Clearinghouse for Science, Mathematics, and Environmental Education, The Ohio State University, 1929 Kenny Rd., Columbus, OH 43210-1080; (614) 292-6717; (800) 276-0462; 800-LET-ERIC (for new users) http://www.ericse.org

Geological Society of America, 3300 Penrose Pl., P.O. Box 9140, Boulder, CO 80301-9140; (303) 447-2020; (800) 472-1988 http://www.geosociety.org

The GLOBE Program, 744 Jackson Pl., NW, Washington, DC 20503; (800) 858-9947 http://www.globe.gov

Great Lakes Planetarium Association (GLPA), c/o D. David Batch, Abrams Planetarium, Michigan State University, East Lansing, MI 48824; (517) 355-4676 http://www.pa.msu.edu/abrams/glpa.html

Harvard-Smithsonian Center for Astrophysics, Science Education Department, 60 Garden St., MS-71, Cambridge, MA 02138; (617) 495-9798 http://cfa-www.harvard.edu/cfa/sed

JASON Project, JASON Foundation for Education, 395 Totten Pond Rd., Waltham, MA 02154; (617) 487-9995 http://www.jasonproject.org

Los Alamos National Laboratory, Box 1663, MS P278, Los Alamos, NM 87545; (505) 667-1919 http://www.education.lanl.gov/resources

Middle Atlantic Planetarium Society (MAPS), c/o Laura Deines, MAPS President, Southworth Planetarium, P.O. Box 9300, Portland, ME 04104-9300; (207) 780-4249 http://www.voicenet.com/~mcdonald/MAPS.html

The Museum Insititute for Teaching Science, 79 Milk St., Suite 210, Boston, MA 02109-3903; (617) 695-9771   http://www.mits.org

National Aeronautics and Space Administration (NASA), Central Operation of Resources for Educators, Lorain County Joint Vocational School, 15181 Rte. 58 S., Oberlin, OH 44074; (216) 774-1051, Ext. 293 and 249 http://spacelink.msfc.nasa.gov/CORE

National Aeronautics and Space Administration (NASA), Education Division, Code FE, NASA Headquarters, 300 E St., SW, Washington, DC 20546; (202) 358-1110 http://www/hq.nasa.gov/office/codef/education

National Aeronautics and Space Administration (NASA), NASA Marshall Space Flight Center, Mail Code CL-01, Huntsville, AL 35812-0001; (205) 961-1225   http://spacelink/nasa.gov

National Association of Biology Teachers, 11250 Roger Bacon Dr., No. 19, Reston, VA 20190-5202; (703) 471-1134; (800) 406-0775

National Center for Improving Science Education, 2000 L St., NW, Suite 603, Washington, DC 20036; (202) 467-0652   http://www.wested.org

National Center for Research on Teacher Learning, Michigan State University, College of Education, 116 Erickson Hall, East Lansing, MI 48824-1034; (517) 355-9302 http://ncrtl.msu.edu

National Energy Foundation, 5225 Wiley Post Way, Suite 170, Salt Lake City, UT 84116; (801) 539-1406   http://www.nef1.org

National Gardening Association, 180 Flynn Ave., Burlington, VT 05401; (802) 863-1308; (800) 538-7476   http://www.garden.org

National Geographic Society, 1145 17th St., NW, Washington, DC 20036; (202) 857-7000; (800) 368-2728 http://www.nationalgeographic.com

National Institute for Science Education, 1025 W. Johnson St., Madison, WI 53706; (608) 263-9250 http://www.wcer.wisc.edu/nise

National Marine Educators Association, P.O. Box 1470, Ocean Springs, MS 39566-1470; (601) 374-7557   http://www.marine-ed.org

National Research Council; Center for Science, Mathematics, and Engineering Education, 2101 Constitution Ave., NW, Washington, DC 20418; (202) 334-2353 http://www2.nas.edu/center

National Science Foundation, Directorate for Education and Human Resources, 4201 Wilson Blvd., Arlington, VA 22230; (703) 306-1600 http://www.ehr.nsf.gov

National Science Foundation, Directorate for Education and Human Resources, Division of Educational System Reform, 4201 Wilson Blvd., Rm. 875, Arlington, VA 22230; (703) 306-1690 http://www.ehr.nsf.gov/ehr/esr

National Science Resources Center, Smithsonian Institution, MRC 403, Arts and Industries Bldg., Rm. 1201, Washington, DC 20560; (202) 357-2555   http://www.si.edu/nsrc

National Science Teachers Association (NSTA), 1840 Wilson Blvd., Arlington, VA 22201-3000; (703) 243-7100   http://www.nsta.org

National Student Research Center, Mandeville Middle School, 2525 Soult St., Mandeville, LA 70448; (504) 626-5980 http://yn.la.ca.us/nsrc/nsrc.html

National Weather Association, 6704 Wolke Ct., Montgomery, AL 36116-2134; (334) 213-0388
http://www.nwas.org

National Wildlife Federation, 8925 Leesburg Pike, Vienna, VA 22184-0001; (703) 790-4000
http://www.nwf.org

Pacific Planetarium Association, c/o Jon Elvert, 2300 Leo Harris Pkwy., Eugene, OR 97401; (541) 687-STAR (program information); (541) 461-8227
http://www.efn.org/~esd_plt

Project WET, The Watercourse Program, 201 Culbertson Hall, Montana State University, Bozeman, MT 59717-0057; (406) 994-5392
http://www.montana.edu/wwwwet

Project WILD, 5430 Grosvenor Lane, Suite 230, Bethesda, MD 20814; (301) 493-5447
http://eelink.umich.edu/wild

Smithsonian Institution, Office of Education, MRC 402, Arts and Industries Bldg., Rm. 1163, Washington, DC 20560; (202) 357-2425
http://educate.si.edu

Soil and Water Conservation Society, 7515 N.E. Ankeny Rd., Ankeny, IA 50021; (515) 289-2331; (800) THE-SOIL   http://www.swcs.org

TERC, 2067 Massachusetts Ave., Cambridge, MA 02140; (617) 547-0430   http://www.terc.edu

U.S. Space Foundation, 2860 S. Circle Dr., Suite 2301, Colorado Springs, CO 80906-4184; (719) 576-8000; (800) 691-4000 http://www.ussf.org

World Wildlife Fund, 1250-24th St., NW, Washington, DC 20037-1175; (202) 293-4800
http://www.wwf.org

Young Astronaut Council, 1308-19th St., NW, Washington, DC 20036; (202) 682-1984
http://www.yac.org

Young Entomologists Society, 1915 Peggy Pl., Lansing, MI 48910-2553; (517) 887-0499
http://insects.ummz.lsa.umich.edu/yes/yes.html

SCIENCE PUBLISHERS AND SUPPLIERS

Active Learning Associates, 520 N. Adams St., Ypsilanti, MI 48197-2482; (800) 993-9499; Fax: (908) 284-0405
http://www.childrenssoftware.com

AIMS Education Foundation, P.O. Box 8120, Fresno, CA 93747-8120; (209) 255-4094; Fax: (209) 255-6396

Air & Space/Smithsonian, P.O. Box 420113, Palm Coast, FL 32142-0113; (800) 766-2149

Air and Waste Management Association (A&WMA), P.O. Box 915, Hudson, NH 03051; (800) 258-1302; Fax: (603) 880-6520

American Association for the Advancement of Science (AAAS), Directorate for Education and Human Resource Programs, 1200 New York Ave., NW, Washington, DC 20005; (202) 326-6454; Fax: (202) 371-9849   http://ehr.aaas.org

American Chemical Society (to order periodicals), P.O. Box 2537, Kearneysville, WV 25430; (800) 209-0423; Fax: (800)525-5562

American Forest Foundation, 1111-19th St., NW, Washington, DC 20036; (202) 463-2462; Fax: (202) 463-2461

American Geological Institute, P.O. Box 205, Annapolis Junction, MD 20701; (301) 953-1744; Fax: (301) 206-9789

American Institute of Mining, Metallurgical and Petroleum Engineers (AIME), 345 E. 47th St., 14th Fl., New York, NY 10017; (212) 705-7695; Fax: (212) 371-9622

American Library Association (to order *Booklist*), 434 W. Downer Pl., Aurora, IL 60506; (800) 542-2433, ext. 5715   http://www.ala.org/booklist

American Library Association (to order *Science Books for Young People*), Order Department, 155 N. Wacker Dr., Chicago, IL 60606; (800) 545-2433

American Museum of Natural History, Education Department, Central Park West at 79th Street, New York, NY 10024; (212) 769-5304; Fax: (212) 769-5329

American Plastics Council, 1801 K St., NW, Suite 701-L, Washington, DC 20006-1301; (800) 243-5790; Fax: (202) 296-7119

American Society of Educators, 1429 Walnut St., Philadelphia, PA 19102; (215) 563-6005; Fax: (215) 587-9706   http://www.media-methods.com

Association of Science-Technology Centers, 1025 Vermont Ave., NW, Suite 500, Washington, DC 20005; (202) 783-7200; Fax: (202) 783-7207 http://www.astc.org/astc

Astronomical Society of the Pacific, 390 Ashton Ave., San Francisco, CA 94112; (800) 335-2624; (415) 337-1100; Fax: (415) 337-5205 www.aspsky.org

Carnegie Corporation of New York, P.O. Box 753, Waldorf, MD 20642

Carolina Biological Supply Co., 2700 York Rd., Burlington, NC 27215-3398; (800) 334-5551; Fax: (800) 222-7112

Carson-Dellosa Publishing Company, P.O. Box 35665, Greensboro, NC 27425-5665; (800) 321-0943; Fax; (800) 535-2669

Chemical Industry Education Centre, University of York, Heslington, York YO1 5DD, United Kingdom; (44-1904) 432600; Fax: (44-1904) 432605   Email: ciec@york.ac.uk

Children's Book Council, 568 Broadway, Suite 404, New York, NY 10012; (212) 966-1990; Fax: (212) 966-2073   http://www.cbcbooks.org

Cobblestone Publishing, 7 School St., Peterborough, NH 03458-1454; (800) 821-0115; (603) 924-7209; Fax: (603) 924-7380

Cornell Instructional Materials Service, Kennedy Hall, Cornell University, Ithaca, NY 14853-4203; (607) 255-9252; Fax: (607) 255-7905

The Cousteau Society, 870 Greenbrier Circle, Suite 402, Chesapeake, VA 23320-9864; (757) 523-9335; Fax: (757) 523-2747

Critical Thinking Books & Software, P.O. Box 448, Pacific Grove, CA 93950-0448; (800) 458-4849; (408) 393-3288; Fax: (408) 393-3277 http://www.criticalthinking.com

Cuisenaire/Dale Seymour Publications, P.O. Box 5026, White Plains, NY 10602-5026; (800) 237-0338; Fax: (800) 551-7637 http://www.cuisenaire.com

Delta Education, P.O. Box 915, Hudson, NH 03501; (800) 258-1302; Fax: (603) 880-6520

Discover, P.O. Box 420105, Palm Coast, FL 32142-0105; (800) 829-9132

Educational Products Information Exchange (EPIE) Institute, 103 W. Montauk Hwy., Suite 3, Hampton Bays, NY 11946; (516) 728-9100; Fax: (516) 728-9228   http://www.epie.org

Electronic Learning, P.O. Box 53896, Boulder, CO 80322; (800) 544-2917

The Exploratorium, 3601 Lyon St., San Francisco, CA 94123; (415) 561-0393; Fax: (415) 561-0307 http://www.exploratorium.edu

Federal Emergency Management Agency, P.O. Box 70274, Washington, DC 20024; (202) 646-3104; Fax: (202) 646-2812

Field Museum of Natural History, Education Department/Books; Roosevelt Road and Lake Shore Drive, Chicago, IL 60605-2496; (312) 922-9410; Fax: (312) 922-6483 http://www.bvis.vic/edu/museum/harris_loan

Flinn Scientific, P.O. Box 219, Batavia, IL 60510; (630) 879-6900; Fax: (630) 879-6962

Franklin Watts, 5440 N. Cumberland Ave., Chicago, IL 60656; (800) 672-6672; Fax: (312) 374-4329

Fulcrum Publishing, 350 Indiana St., Suite 350, Golden, CO 80401-5093; (800) 992-2908; Fax: (800) 726-7112 htttp://www.fulcrum-books.com

Geothermal Education Office, 664 Hilary Dr., Tiburon, CA 94920; (800) 866-4436; Fax: (415) 435-7737

Glencoe/McGraw-Hill, P.O. Box 543, Blacklick, OH 43004-9902; (800) 334-7344; Fax: (614) 860-1877

Globe Fearon, 4350 Equity Dr., P.O. Box 2649, Columbus, OH 43216; (800) 848-9500; Fax: (614) 771-7361

Good Year Books, 299 Jefferson Rd., P.O. Box 480, Parsippany, NJ 07054-0480; (800) 321-3106

Grolier Publishing, Sherman Turnpike, Danbury, CT 06813; (800) 621-1115; Fax: (312) 374-4329

Harcourt Brace and Company, 6277 Sea Harbor Dr., Orlando, FL 32887; (800) 782-4479; Fax: (800) 874-6418

Heinemann, 361 Hanover St., Portsmouth, NH 03801-3912; (800) 541-2086; (603) 431-7894; Fax: (800) 847-0938   http://www.heinemann.com

Heldref Publications, 1319-18th St., NW, Washington, DC 20036-1802; (800) 365-9753; (202) 296-6267; Fax: (202) 296-5149

Holt, Rinehart and Winston, 6277 Sea Harbor Dr., Orlando, FL 32887; (800) 782-4479; Fax: (800) 874-6418

Houghton Mifflin Company, 181 Ballardvale St., Box 7050, Wilmington, MA 01887; (800) 225-3362; Fax: (800) 634-7568

Idea Factory, 10710 Dixon Dr., Riverview, FL 33569; (800) 331-6204; Fax: (813) 677-0373

Incentive Publications, 3835 Cleghorn Ave., Nashville, TN 37215; (800) 421-2830; (615) 385-2967

Institute for Chemical Education, Department of Chemistry, University of Wisconsin, 1101 University Ave., Madison, WI 53706-1396; (608) 262-3033; Fax: (608) 262-0381

International Society for Technology in Education, Customer Service Office, 480 Charnelton St., Eugene, OR 97401-2626; (800) 336-5191; Fax: (541) 302-3778 Email: cust_svc@ccmail.uoregon.edu

International Technology Education Association, 1914 Association Dr., Suite 201, Reston, VA 20191-1539; (703) 860-2100; Fax: (703) 860-0353 hhtp://www.iteawww.org

Issues in Science and Technology, Circulation Services, P.O. Box 661, Holmes, PA 19043-9699; (214) 883-6325 http://www.utdallas.edu/research/issues

J. Weston Walch, 321 Valley St., P.O. Box 658, Portland, ME 04104-0658; (800) 341-6094; Fax: (207) 772-3105

Kalmbach Publishing Co., 21027 Crossroads Circle, P.O. Box 1612, Waukesha, WI 53187; (800) 553-6644; (414) 796-8776; Fax: (414) 796-0126 http://www.kalmbach.com

Karol Media, 350 N. Pennsylvania Ave., P.O. Box 7600, Wilkes-Barre, PA 18773-7600; (800) 526-4773; Fax: (717) 822-8226

Kendall/Hunt Publishing Co., 4050 Westmark Dr., Dubuque, IA 52002; (800) 542-6657; Fax: (800) 772-9165   http://www.kendallhunt.com

Kids Discover, P.O. Box 54205, Boulder, CO 80322; (800) 284-8276

Lab-Aids, 17 Colt Ct., Ronkonkoma, NY 11779; (516) 737-1133; Fax: (516) 737-1286

LaMotte Co., P.O. Box 329, Chestertown, MD 21620; (800) 344-3100; Fax: (410) 778-6394

Lawrence Erlbaum Associates, 10 Industrial Ave., Mahwah, NJ 07430-2262; (800) 9-BOOKS-9 (for orders only); (201) 236-9500; Fax: (201) 236-0072 http://www.erlbaum.com

Lawrence Hall of Science, LHS GEMS, University of California, Berkeley, CA 94720-5200; (510) 642-7771; Fax: (510) 643-0309

Learning Innovations, 91 Montvale Ave., Stoneham, MA 02180; (781) 279-8214; Fax: (781) 279-8220

The Learning Team, 84 Business Park Rd., Armonk, NY 10504; (800) 793-TEAM; Fax: (914) 273-2227

LEGO Dacta, 555 Taylor Rd., P.O. Box 1600, Enfield, CT 06083-1600; (800) 527-8339; Fax: (203) 763-2466

Library of Congress, Science and Technology Division, Science Reference Section, 10 First St., SE, Washington, DC 20540-5580 gopher://marvel.loc.gov.70/11/research/ readingrooms/science/bibs.guides/tracer

McGraw Hill Publishing Co., 220 East Danieldale Rd., DeSoto, TX 75115; (800) 442-9685; (214) 224-1111; Fax: (214) 228-1982

Millbrook Press, P.O. Box 335, Brookfield, CT 06804; (800) 462-4703; Fax: (203) 740-2223

Miller Freeman, P.O. Box 5052, Vandalia, OH 45377; (701) 777-2864 http://www.techlearning.com

Morrow Junior Books, 1350 Avenue of the Americas, New York, NY 10019; (800) 843-9389; Fax: (212) 261-6689

NASCO, 901 Janesville Ave., Fort Atkinson, WI 53538-0901; (800) 558-9595; (414) 563-2446; Fax: (414) 563-8296

National Academy Press, 2101 Constitution Ave., NW, Lockbox 285, Washington, DC 20055; (800) 624-6242; (202) 334-3313; Fax: (202) 334-2451   http://www.nap.edu/bookstore

National Air and Space Museum, Educational Services Department, Smithsonian, MRC-305, Washington, DC 20560; (202) 786-2101; Fax: (202) 633-8928

National Aquarium in Baltimore, Education Department, 501 E. Pratt St., Pier 3, Baltimore, MD 21202; (410) 576-3870; Fax: (410) 659-0116

National Association of Geoscience Education, P.O. Box 5443, Bellingham, WA 98227-5443; (360) 650-3587; (360) 650-3582; Fax: (360) 650-7302 Email: xman@henson.cc.wwu.edu

National Audubon Society, Membership Data Center, P.O. Box 52529, Boulder, CO 80322; (800) 274-4201; Fax: (303) 604-7455

National Center for Improving Science Education, 2000 L St., NW, Suite 616, Washington, DC 20036; (202) 467-0652; Fax: (202) 467-0659 Email: info@ncise.org

National Energy Information Center, Foresstal Bldg.—EI-30, 1000 Independence Ave., SW, Washington, DC 20585; (202) 586-8800; Fax: (202) 586-0727   http://eia.doe.gov

National 4-H Supply Service, 7100 Connecticut Ave., Chevy Chase, MD 20815; (301) 961-2934; Fax: (301) 961-2937

National Middle School Association, 2600 Corporate Exchange Dr., Suite 370, Columbus, OH 43231-1672; (614) 895-4730; Fax: (614) 895-4750

National Technical Information Service (NTIS), Springfield, VA 22161; (800) 553-6847; Fax: (703) 321-8547   http://www.ntis.gov

NOAA/ERL/FSL (National Oceanic and Atmospheric Administration, Environmental, Research Laboratories, Forecast Systems Laboratory), 325 Broadway, Mail Code REFS, Boulder, CO 80303; (303) 497-6045; Fax: (303) 497-6064

Oryx Press, 4041 N. Central Ave., Suite 700, Phoenix, AZ 85012-3397; (800) 279-6799; (602) 265-2651; Fax: (800) 279-4663 http://www.oryxpress.com

Oxford University Press, 2001 Evans Rd., Cary, NC 27513; (800) 451-7556; Fax (919) 677-1303 http://www.oup-usa.org

PLANETS Educational Technology Systems, P.O. Box 22477, San Diego, CA 92192-2477; (619) 587-2138

Polystrene Packaging Council, 1801 K St., NW, Suite 600K, Washington, DC 20036; (202) 974-5341; Fax: (202) 296-7354   http://www.polystrene.org

Popular Science, Box 5100, Harlan, IA 51537; (212) 779-5000

Prentice Hall/Allyn & Bacon, 200 Old Tappan Rd. Old Tappan, NJ 07675; (800) 223-1360

Sargent-Welch/VWR Scientific, 911 Commerce Ct., P.O. Box 5229, Buffalo Grove, IL 60089-5229; (800) 727-4368; Fax: (800) 676-2540 http://www.sargentwelch.com

Scholastic, Instructional Publishing Group, 555 Broadway, New York, NY 10012; (212) 343-6100

School Library Journal, P.O. Box 57559, Boulder, CO 80322-7559; (800) 456-9409; Fax: (800) 824-4746

Science Books & Films, Department SBF, P.O. Box 3000, Denville, NJ 07834; (202) 326-6454; Fax: (202) 371-9849

Science Service, Subscriptions Department, P.O. Box 1925, Marion, OH 43305; (800) 247-2160; Fax: (614) 382-5866   http://sciencenews.org

Scientific American, P.O. Box 3186, Harlan, IA 51593-2377; (212) 355-0408 http://www.sciam.com

Scientific American Frontiers School Program, 105 Terry Dr., Suite 120, Newtown, PA 18940-3425; (800) 314-5010; Fax: (215) 579-8589 http://www.pbs.org/saf

Scott Foresman/Addison-Wesley, 1 Jacob Way, Reading, MA 01867; (800) 552-2259; Fax: (800) 333-3328   http://www.sf.aw.com

Sea World of Florida, Education Department, 7007 Sea World Dr., Orlando, FL 32821; (407) 351-3600; Fax: (407) 363-2399

Silver Burdett Ginn, Education School Group, P.O. Box 2649, Columbus, OH 43216; (800) 848-9500; Fax: (614) 771-7361

Sky and Telescope, P.O. Box 9111, Belmont, MA 02178-9917; (800) 253-0245; Fax: (617) 864-6117 http://www.skypub.com

Springer-Verlag New York, P.O. Box 2485, Secaucus, NJ 07096-2485; (800) 777-4643; (201) 348-4033 (in New York); Fax: (201) 348-4505

StarDate, 2609 University Ave., Rm. 3-118, The University of Texas at Austin, Austin, TX 78712; (800) STA-RDATE; (512) 471-5285; Fax: (512) 471-5060   http://pio.as.utexas.edu

Superintendent of Documents, U.S. Government Printing Office, P.O. Box 371954, Pittsburgh, PA 15240-7954; (202) 512-1800; Fax: (202) 512-2250

Teacher Created Materials, P.O. Box 1040, Huntington Beach, CA 92647; (800) 662-4321; (714) 891-7895   http://www.teachercreated.com

Teacher Ideas Press, P.O. Box 6633, Englewood, CO 80155-6633; (800) 237-6124; Fax: (303) 220-8843 http://www.lu.com

Teachers College Press, Teachers College, Columbia University, 1234 Amsterdam Ave., New York, NY 10027; (212) 678-3929; Fax: (212) 678-4149 http://www.tc.columbia.edu/~tcpress

Teacher's Laboratory, P.O. Box 6480, Brattleboro, VT 05302-6480; (800) 769-6199; Fax: (802) 254-5233   Email: connect@sover.net

3-2-1 Contact Magazine, P.O. Box 51177, Boulder CO 80322-1177; (800) 678-0613

Tom Snyder Productions, 80 Coolidge Hill Rd., Watertown, MA 02172-2817; (800) 342-0236; Fax: (617) 926-6222

TOPS Learning Systems, 10970 S. Mulino Rd., Canby, OR 97013; (503) 266-8550; Fax: (503) 266-5200

UCAR LEARN Center, P.O. Box 3000, Boulder, CO 80307-3000; (303) 497-8107; Fax: (303) 497-8610

UCS Publications, Two Brattle Square, Cambridge, MA 02238-9105; (617) 547-5552; Fax: (617) 864-9405   Email: ucs@ucsusa.org

U.S. Environmental Protection Agency, Office of Research and Development, 401 M St., SW, Washington, DC 20460; (202) 260-8619; Fax: (202) 260-4095

U.S. Forest Service, Intermountain Region, Public Affairs Office, 324-25th St., Ogden, UT 85501; (801) 625-5827; Fax: (801) 625-5240 http://www.fs.fed.us/outdoors/mrce/iye/contents.html

Wards Natural Science Establishment, P.O. Box 92912, Rochester, NY 14692-9012; (800) 962-2660; Fax: (800) 635-8439

WGBN Boston, Attn: Pring and Outreach, 125 Western Ave., Boston, MA 02134; (617) 492-2777, Ext. 3848; Fax: (617) 787-1639

SCIENCE RESOURCE GUIDES

Berman, Sally. 1993. *Catch Them Thinking Science: A Handbook of Classroom Strategies.* Palantine, IL: IRI/Skylight.

Butzow, Carol M., and John W. Butzow. 1994. *Intermediate Science through Children's Literature: Over Land and Sea.* Englewood, CO: Teacher Ideas Press.

Caduto, Michael J., and Joseph Bruchac. 1991. *Keepers of the Animals: Native American Stories and Wildlife Activities for Children.* Golden, CO: Fulcrum Publishing.

Caduto, Michael J., and Joseph Bruchac. 1994. *Keepers of Life: Discovering Plants Through Native American Stories and Earth Activities for Children.* Golden, CO: Fulcrum Publishing.

DeVito, Alfred, and Gerald H. Krockover. (2000). *The New Activities Handbook for Energy Education.* Parsippany, NJ: Pearson Learning/Good Year Books.

Jewett, John W., Jr. 1994. *Physics Begins with an M...Mysteries, Magic, and Myth.* Boston, MA: Allyn and Bacon.

Kramer, David C. 1989. *Animals in the Classroom: Selection, Care, and Observations.* Parsippany, NJ: Innovative Learning Publications.

Miller, Elizabeth B. 1997. *The Internet Resource Directory for K–12 Teachers and Librarians: 96/97 Edition.* Englewood, CO: Libraries Unlimited.

National Science Resources Center. 1996. *Resources for Teaching Elementary School Science.* Washington, DC: National Academy Press.

National Science Resources Center. 1997. *Science for All Children: A Guide to Improving Elementary Science Education in Your School District.* Washington, DC: National Academy Press.

National Science Resource Center. 1998. *Resources for Teaching Middle School Science.* Washington, DC: National Academy Press.

Phelan, Carolyn. 1996. *Science Books for Young People.* Chicago, IL: American Library Association, Booklist Publications.

Rowe, Mary Budd. 1993. *Science Helper K–8: Version 3.0.* Armonk, NY: The Learning Team.

Science Curriculum Resource Handbook: A Practical Guide for K–12 Science Curriculum. 1992. Millwood, NY: Kraus International Publications.

Stahl, Robert J., ed. 1996. *Cooperative Learning in Science: A Handbook for Teachers.* Parsippany, NJ: Innovative Learning Publications.

Voris, Helen H., Maija Sedzielarz, and Carolyn P. Blackmon. 1986. *Teach the Mind, Touch the Spirit: A Guide to Focused Field Trips.* Chicago, IL: Field Museum of Natural History, Department of Education.

Walthall, Barbara, ed. 1995. *IDEAAAS: Sourcebook for Science, Mathematics and Technology Education.* Washington, DC: American Association for the Advancement of Science; Armonk, NY: The Learning Team.

Watts, Mike. 1991. *The Science of Problem-Solving: A Practical Guide for Science Teachers.* Portsmouth, NH: Heinemann.

Weisberger, Robert A. 1995. *Science Success for Students with Disabilities.* Parsippany, NJ: Innovative Learning Publications.

Wolfson, Michelle. 1993. Resources for Teaching Astronomy and Space Science. John Hewitt, ed. In *Planetarium Activities for Student Success.* Vol. 3. Berkeley, CA: Lawrence Hall of Science; Flushing Meadows, Corona Park, NY: New York Hall of Science.

Wood, Clair G. 1995. *Safety in School Science Labs.* Natick, MA: James A. Kaufman & Associates.